Heinrich Schipperges
The World of Hildegard of Bingen

Heinrich Schipperges

THE WORLD OF
HILDEGARD OF BINGEN
Her Life, Times, and Visions

Translated by John Cumming

BURNS & OATES

NOVALIS

First published in this translation in 1998 by
BURNS & OATES,
Wellwood, North Farm Road,
Tunbridge Wells, Kent TN2 3DR

Published in the United States of America by
THE LITURGICAL PRESS,
St John's Abbey, Collegeville,
Minnesota 56321

Published in Canada by
NOVALIS
49 Front Street, Second Floor,
Toronto, Ontario M5E 1B3

Original German edition: *Die Welt von Hildegard von Bingen*,
Copyright © 1997 Verlag Herder, Freiburg im Breisgau, Germany

ISBN 0 86012 284 0   Burns & Oates
ISBN 0-8146-2543-6   The Liturgical Press
ISBN 2-89088-987-4   Novalis

Canadian Cataloguing in Publication Data

Schipperges, Heinrich
     The world of Hildegard of Bingen: her life, times, and visions

Translation of : Die Welt von Hildegard von Bingen.
Includes bibliographical references and index.
ISBN 2-89088-987-4 (Novalis) — ISBN 0-86012-284-0 (Burns &
     Oates) — ISBN 0-8146-2542-6 (Liturgical Press)

     1. Hildegard, Saint, 1098–1179. 2. Christian saints—
Germany—Biography. 3. Women mystics—Germany—
Biography. I. Cumming, John. II. Title.

BX4700.H5S2713 1998   282'.092   C98-900847-9

Picture Editor: Birgit Wiesenhütter
Design: Finken & Bumiller, Stuttgart

Jacket front illustration: *Angelic Choir* (detail)
Liber Scivias, copy of the former Rupertsberg Codex, *c.* 1180,
St Hildegard's Abbey, Eibingen

Printed in Spain by Elkar S. Coop. Bilbao 48012

Contents

Introduction

Hildegard of Bingen was abbess and healer, politician and prophet, saint and theologian. She was uniquely devout, intelligent and well-informed in many fields. Above all she was a visionary: a celebrant of great mysteries. Her words are as packed with imagery as her pictures. When we first see, read or listen to her creations, the world they portray and lead us into may seem very odd and even mysterious, but as we make our way through it with the help of this extraordinary woman, we shall begin to understand much of its nature and, above all, discover its vital relevance to us and to the way we live now.

Of course the actual world Hildegard lived in bears little outward resemblance to our own at the dawn of the third millennium. So many eras and movements, the Renaissance and the Reformation, humanism and the Enlightenment, idealism and positivism, and even the utopian vistas of Post-modernism, to name only some major phases of the centuries in between, separate the twelfth century from our own times.

Clearly we cannot plunge into Hildegard's inner world, or haphazardly extract this or that fragment of it for contemplation, without any real idea of the age in which she lived and of its dramatic changes and upheavals. Only if we appreciate something of the peculiar tension between tradition and reform that was characteristic of her external world in so many of its manifestations can we grasp the significance of Hildegard's life and achievements and especially of their visionary and prophetic aspects. Then we shall see that the way in which she saw and understood humanity is the key to what she has to say about nature and healing. In the next stage of our journey with Hildegard, her concept of the world and of the function and fate of human beings in it will take us into the mysteries of creation and redemption. By then we shall have a very good idea of the original setting of Hildegard's thoughts about active healing, which now seem astonishingly up-to-date in so many respects but can only gain in power and impact after the mental journey that I have outlined.

Obviously the world of Hildegard of Bingen means much more than the world in which she lived in a purely chronological sense, and of course much more than her immediate physical surroundings. Most of all, for us, it is the world as she experienced it with such feeling and tried in her own way to shape as joy and vitality. In this Hildegardian world human beings are responsible not only for their own lives and personal happiness but for their fellow humans, for the environment, for the world of the future, and indeed for the universe as a whole. Of course we have to adopt this general way of seeing things, or an approximation to it, in order to grasp the real significance of anything of lasting value in the writing and art of the Middle Ages. But its concentrated truth and relevance are the very essence of Hildegard's message, however various the cosmic imagery in which she conveys it, and however dramatic the history of salvation that provides its underlying strength and sense of purpose.

Accordingly, this book offers not so much a picture of the world as a world of images, verbal, conceptual, pictorial, and creative, which the many illustrations help us to visualize appropriately. They should not only illuminate a world for the most part lost and alien to very many of us, but, like Hildegard, shed their own powerful light in the midst of our own world which, for all its cult of the image, is visually impoverished as far as true perception and insight are concerned.

Heinrich Schipperges
Heidelberg, 1997

Abbreviations

PL   "S. Hildegardis Abbatissae Opera"
(Collected Works), J.-P. Migne, ed., in
Patrologia Latina, vol. 197 (Paris,1882).

Pi   *Analecta Sacra*, vol. 8, J. B. Pitra, ed.
(Monte Cassino, 1882).

Sc   "Scivias," in *Patrologia Latina*, vol. 197,
cc. 383-738.

LVM   "Liber Vitae Meritorum" (The Book of
Life's Merits), in *Analecta Sacra*, pp. 1-
244.

CaCu   *Hildegardis Causae et Curae* (Hildegard's
Causes and Cures), P. Kaiser, ed.
(Leipzig, 1903).

V   *Vita Sanctae Hildegardis auctoribus
Godefrido et Theodorico monachis* (The
life of St Hildegard by the monks
Godfrey and Theodoric). In Patrologia
Latina, vol.197, cc. 115-30.

Bw   *Briefwechsel* (Correspondence). German
translation from the oldest surviving
manuscripts by Adelgundis Führkötter
(Salzburg, 1965).

S   Hildegard von Bingen, *Symphonia.
Gedichte und Gesänge* (Poems, Hymns
and Songs), Walter Berschin and
Heinrich Schipperges, eds (Gerlingen,
1995).

1. An age of upheaval

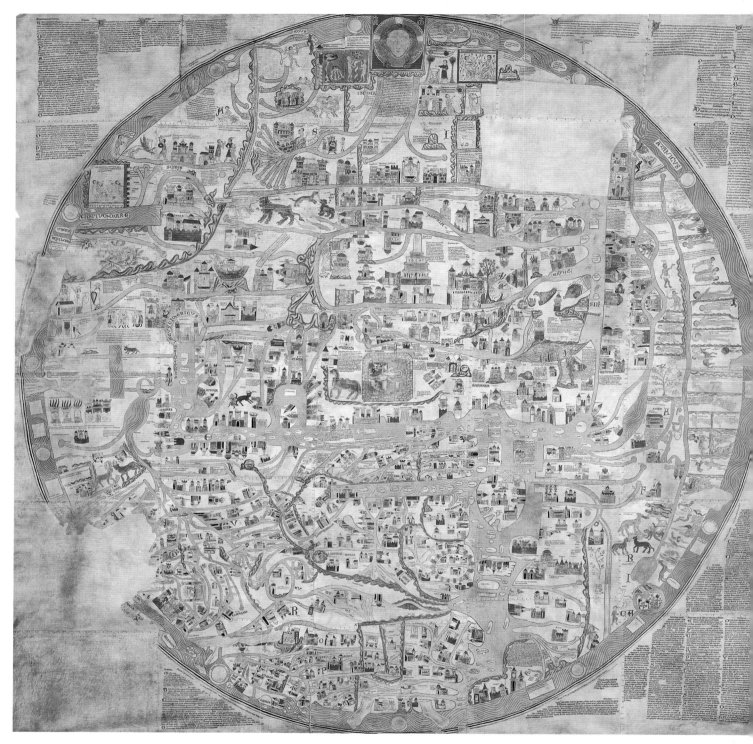

1. The Ebstorf Map of the World

13th century, original destroyed

The Ebstorf Map of the World is the most detailed and important of surviving representations of the known and imagined world from the European Middle Ages. The map measures 3.5 x 3.5 metres and shows Asia, Europe, and Africa in a circle with Jerusalem as the central point. It features about 1,500 drawings and explanatory texts and is a unique compendium of universal knowledge in the high Middle Ages. The map depicts the surface of the earth as a theatre of mythical, biblical, and historical events. It is not only a major work of cartography but offers a consistent understanding of the world.

The world and life of the twelfth century

"Who is this woman", asked Pope Eugenius III of Hildegard of Bingen, "who rises out of the wilderness like a column of smoke from burning spices?" The twelfth century, compared with preceding centuries, hardly seems like a wilderness as we look back on it and try to grasp it as a whole. It gave rise to a new, astonishingly rich and complex world. It was the high point of the period deservedly known as the High Middle Ages. The German (or Holy Roman) Emperor and the Pope were marking out the limits of their particular domains within a surprisingly extensive Europe. It had fluid borders to the east and to the west that allowed a two-way traffic to and from the periphery of the effectively known world. Extremely varied forms of international trade linked the Europe of Latin Christianity with Byzantium, the Rome of the east, and with Islamic Iberia. Latin itself had become the language not only of the Church but of the Holy Roman Empire and of cultivated Europe in every sense.

It was also an age of upheaval, and of new formations and enthusiasms. The realm of the intellect (*Studium*) was staking out its own claim, as it were, between the areas over which the Empire (*Imperium*) and the Church (*Sacerdotium*) held sway. Once again the scholar came into his own alongside the knight and the monk. Learning was the great new spiritual force of the Christian West in the twelfth century.

But the same century also experienced the onset of a larger time-span, that of the versatile yet contradictory era which heralded not only the rise of Europe but the decline of the West. The twelfth century may be thought of as the interface between two ages. It certainly experienced epoch-making processes most readily perceptible in an economic realignment of society, a shift in the power and influence of the different social "estates," and a burgeoning of intellectual and spiritual movements. The concurrent revaluation of work led to a new interest in the scope of human action. The "mechanical arts" (*Artes mechanicae*), agriculture and architecture, hunting and fishing, the activities of mills and workshops, gardening and cooking, as well as practical medicine with its connections with all the arts, moved to a new position alongside the "liberal arts" (*Artes liberales*).

New forms of agrarian economy led to an increased yield from the land. Hitherto untouched areas were opened up to cultivation, and novel forms of tenure were devised. Feudal bonds began to slacken. Long-distance commerce started to flourish, and trade and crafts prospered. The towns grew stronger, and their citizens found ever more effective ways of asserting their rights and opinions. Scholars moved from one school to another. Troubadours in the well-established Provençal tradition spread over the whole of Europe. Even the mystics of the twelfth century were not ineffectual solitaries, for their insights and writings found a growing audience and inspired many followers.

The human environment

In spite of all these developments, the world of the early twelfth century into which Hildegard was born to Hildebert and Mechthild, in her father's manor-house on his Bermersheim estate near Alzey, Rheinhessen, was still largely one of country pursuits. She spent the first years of her life in an extensive landscape where the main observable activities were those of peasants and farmers.

Whatever primary sources we consult, whether early annals, chronicles, the narratives and tales known as "Gesta," or the works of such historians as Widukind and Thietmar, Adam von Bremen and Otto Freising, we constantly come across the basic agricultural activities of early western Europe that largely decided and shaped the everyday life of the majority of its people.

The "world" as human beings conceived of it at that time was very clear, direct and easy to grasp as a consistent whole. The earth was surrounded by a continuous expanse of water; it floated, so to speak, on the ocean like a vast and marvellous ship. That is something like the world as depicted in the vast—three and a half metres in diameter— dimensions of the altar-piece painted for the Benedictine monastery of Ebstorf in the Lüneberg Heath area of northern Germany. It is a gigantic map of the world at the beginning of the thirteenth century, with the earth as the Body of Christ, Jerusalem as the centre-point, and everything oriented to the east, which is dominated by Christ's head to denote the spiritual illumination of the whole, on which the sun, also rising there, bestows its physical light.

The medieval earth is predominantly a land mass surrounded and veined by water. Even the mountains look like heavy walls separating one country from another. Palestine, of course, appears bigger than Greece, and even Carthage, which had disappeared long before, is shown, whereas London, for instance, is missing. The Garden of Eden has been tucked in between the Ganges and the Caucasus. The Ebstorf map of the world also shows Adam and Eve enjoying the Forbidden Fruit. We can even see the remains of the Tower of Babel, and Noah's Ark is perched on Mount Ararat, for this is a world of memories and insights and above all a Land of Promise.

The world is vast and the heavens broad. We are shown the moon making its peaceful way around the earth. Seven planetary spheres are always visible. All this lies within the infinite, or rather seamless, circumference of the starry firmament, the confines of space. The foregoing is the sole, fixed, all-embracing reality of the Middle Ages. It is a world long ago surrendered by our forebears and therefore by us. Nevertheless, every day of our lives we still experience the rising and going down of the sun, the expansiveness of the earth we walk on, and the ways in which horizons and prospects physical, mental, and spiritual open up to us

only in accordance with our learning and experience, and with our willingness to learn and experience more, and more variously.

The exciting vitality of Europe as it came into existence depended to a great extent on the consistent practice of an essentially agrarian civil society. Agriculture was interwoven with an equally reliable set of processes that determined the setting and structures of daily life: birth and death, labour and celebration, hunger and need, suffering and its management and even defeat. All this took place in conformity with the seasons of the year, the sowing and harvesting of the fruits of the earth, the life and death of animals, the operations of work, and the observance of feast-days, in a continuously recurrent calendar of processes and occasions (*calendarium perpetuum*).

Hildegard of Bingen spent her entire life in the perspective of this fundamentally agricultural society: as a girl on her parents' holding; as an enlightened nun on the land of the Disibodenberg and Rupertsberg monasteries; as a responsible abbess riding along the lanes and roads of Germany not only to carry out her formal duties but on preaching tours; as a sought-after consultant to emperor and popes; as the "Rhineland prophetess," or Sibyl; and as the "Jewel of Bingen" bringing illumination to very different parts of Europe.

Yet Hildegard's works constantly betray her surprisingly low opinion of herself as *indocta*, "unlearned," and without the benefits of an academic structure or "curriculum." This seems all the more uncalled-for when Hildegard at every stage showed herself to be not only highly-cultivated and intellectually proficient but the possessor of a truly profound mind capable of exceptional achievements. She was a woman of the high Middle Ages who had mastered not only theology but contemporary philosophy. That was extraordinary enough. But she was also well versed in the natural sciences and medicine, an expert in husbandry and fish breeding and in the properties of precious stones, and knowledgeable about, say, underwater lore not merely for its own sake but for such practical purposes as healing.

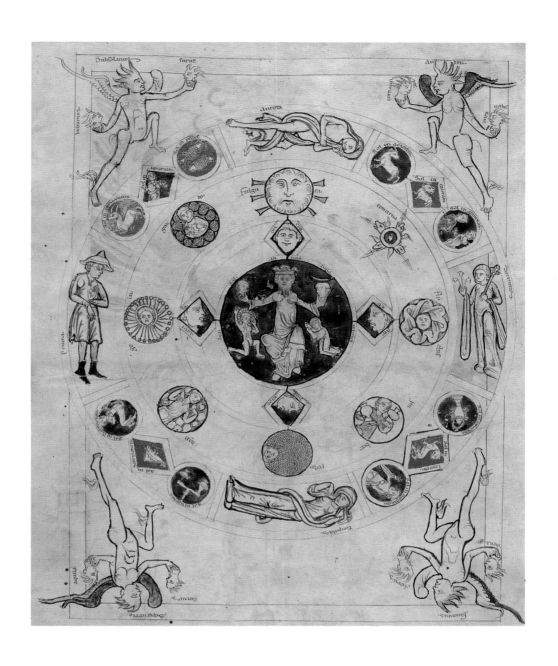

2. An Image of the Year
A picture not only of
"space" but of "time" in the
symbolic form of a
perpetual calendar

Salem Scivias Codex,
13th century
Cod. Sal. X 16, fol. 2v
Heidelberg, University
Library.

13

3. **Septem Artes Liberales**
In the 12th century the seven "arts and sciences" still comprised the traditional system of education in which
Hildegard was trained. Herrad of Landsperg's *Hortus Deliciarum* (Garden of Delights), produced *c.* 1170

A time of upheaval

When we describe the twelfth century as an age of upheaval, we naturally think of the ways in which bondsmen, serfs, and near-serfs left the lower orders and strata of a primarily peasant population and people who were initially vassals came to hold responsible offices in their own right. In addition to such instances of social upheaval the kind of change we are concerned with in the twelfth century is above all the process by which a new stress was placed on reason in scholastic philosophy, and thinkers were liberated, as it were, from another set of no less constrictive bonds: those of unchanging formulas and attitudes of belief. It is highly significant that at the very time (1140) when Abelard was writing his "Know yourself" (*Scito te ipsum*), the nun Hildegard was starting to spread the ideas of her work "Know the ways of the Lord" (*Sci vias Domini*).

Far-sighted men such as Peter the Venerable (Petrus Venerabilis) had already instigated a certain amount of intellectual controversy. Religious centres like Cluny (in France) and St Gallen (in Switzerland) had produced comprehensive and systematic cultural models for others to imitate and adapt. The wandering scholars of the time encouraged people to learn foreign languages and thus provided the essential basis for adopting key aspects of other cultures. Jewish scholars acted as important mediators between hitherto distant complexes of thought not only by drawing attention to eastern sources but by spreading the results once they were assimilated in the West. It was no accident that one of the features common to the writings of the three major religions, Judaism, Islam and Christianity, was an emphasis on the knowledge of nature and on the art of healing as well as due attention to basic philosophical questions.

In this fascinatingly complex world of exciting new developments and, of course, tensions Hildegard did not live the life of a withdrawn if sensitive nun, concentrating only on her monastery garden. On the contrary: she was extraordinarily active and outward-going, in her correspondence and in her public appearances. Hildegard would write to a suppressed nunnery as openly and directly as to a philosophy professor in Paris. She addressed the Emperor Barbarossa as sharply as she did the Cologne clergy. She preached in public, not only in convents but in the market squares of towns and cities. As her biographer reminds us, in all her public appearances Hildegard offered "sound teaching," health-giving knowledge and advice derived from a sophisticated philosophy of the body that was explicitly and meaningfully opposed to the many alternative or heretical doctrines of the period, such as the ultimately destructive dualism of the Cathars and Waldensians, Berengar of Tours' rationalist notion of the sacraments, or Arnold of Brescia's anti-authoritarian theories and practices.

Hildegard the visionary knew that the orthodox, basic Christian understanding of the Incarnation and Resurrection implied that matter and the body were fundamentally real and significant. Accordingly she opposed vague and woolly ideas; and her view of physical reality was clear and consistent but not restrictive. On the contrary, she was open and receptive to experience in a way that would scarcely be possible in later Christian centuries. The salvation or "salving," the health or completeness, of the whole human being was at stake.

Hildegard's idea of the structure of human life was "holistic." It was concentrated on wholeness. She believed that salvation, health, and healing in the earthly realm or the kingdom of the world (*in regno mundi*), were absolutely inseparable from salvation, health, and healing in the divine realm or the kingdom of Christ (*in regno Christi*). Any other way of looking at things, one that missed the vital connections between them, ignored the meaningful structure of the whole, and saw this or that aspect of life out of context was for her "tepid" or "arid," even a "typical woman's" view of nature. "The tree of humanity as I see it now is barren," she wrote to Archbishop Hillin of Trier, "and the world is facing immense dangers. We are up against half-hearted and typically effeminate times. In fact the present age is very like the one in which the first woman deceived the first man." For Hildegard it was a time when a fatal indifference to what really mattered, coupled with a lack of balance and commitment, laid people dangerously open to an immense number of temptations and made them potential victims of deceit, illusion, and error. As she goes on to say: "Unfortunately there is no denying that

the present age is neither cold nor hot, but just tepid." Things would get even worse, however, if "wayward and unmanageable people allow crass and mistaken ideas to blow in on all four winds" (PL 167 B/C).

Hildegard appealed to popes and bishops, kings and the emperor himself to stand up for truth and justice, or implored them merely to look at exactly what was happening and to realize what the outcome might be. "Take a long, hard look at the times you are living in," she wrote to King Conrad III. "They are as giddy and fickle as a woman. They are moving inevitably towards injustice of so extreme and wanton a kind that even the justice of the Lord's own vineyards is threatened with destruction. We have entered a truly calamitous age when God's own precincts begin to reek with the acrid smoke of sorrow and affliction. Not only are the riches of the Church squandered, but the sacred estate itself is mauled as if by a pack of wolves and driven from its own home and mother country. What will all this lead to? To a vast number of people being forced into harsh solitude, to eke out their days serving God in poverty, profound remorse, and deep humiliation. And there is more to come. The mood of these

16

times is degrading enough, but there are yet others on the horizon that menace us with their own brand of misery and wrongdoing" (Bw 81).

Hildegard wrote to Pope Anastasius IV (who reigned from 12 July 1153 to 3 December 1154) with all the forceful conviction of her visions and intuitions: "The entire earth is confused and out of joint under the pressure of a constant flood of false ideas and doctrines, because human beings love what God has already condemned. And you, Rome, are just lying there like someone waiting to die. Can't you see that all the strength of the feet you have stood on so firmly for so long is being sapped and that they will soon give way under you? The trouble is that you have no burning love of justice but approve of it implicitly—in your sleep, that is! Your sheer numbness allows justice to slip away unnoticed." The world, she said, was full of negativity and waste, of excess and dissipation: "For the eye steals, the nose snuffs up and snuffs out, and the mouth kills, whereas healing and salvation come from the heart. The unparalleled light of a new dawn, new desire and new enthusiasm depend on the saving work of the heart" (Bw 40).

Then Hildegard the prophetess subjects the eighty-year-old, tired, all but ineffectual Pope, who had allowed inadequate and corrupt people to hold powerful positions in the Church, to a veritable onslaught of criticism and warnings: "You just have to realize, man, that your powers of perception have grown weak and that you are too worn-out to curb the arrogant boastful behaviour of those in your charge!" She demands: "Why don't you stop these destructive men? Why not pull up these evil roots? Why are you so indifferent to Justice, your 'Heavenly Bride' and the King's own Daughter?" Justice was being ravished "by the immorality of people howling like dogs, and squawking as inanely as chickens in the middle of the night.... Why do you permit these people to lead such licentious lives? Can't you see that they are just staggering around in the darkness of their own stupidity, no better than hens that screech out at night, alerting the robbers to their prey and making their own fate inevitable?" (Bw 39).

The Concordat or Agreement of Worms (1132) seemed to promise an end to the Investiture Controversy in Germany and Italy. The problem of investiture, by which a

monarch granted titles, possessions, and temporal rights to bishops, abbots, and other spiritual lords bedevilled relations between sovereigns and the papacy in the Middle Ages. In 1075 Pope Gregory VII had forbidden lay investiture, or the appointment of lay princes and nobles to sees and prelacies, and started a conflict between the Emperor and the Holy See. Although the Worms Concordat was ratified by the Church at the First Lateran Council (1123), the discussions and quarrels about lay investiture, simony, and the marriage of priests did not cease.

In this respect Hildegard wanted a straight-forward separation of spiritual and secular power, which she took to be the undoubted will of God (*jussit, ut isti pallium, illi tunica tribueretur*: "As far as God is concerned, a spiritual lord is invested with sacred things, and a secular lord with secular things"). "The clergy should have what is due to them and the same goes for non-clerics." In that case (she asked), how could all those men plainly distinguished by their clerical tonsures justify having not only soldiers and weapons but more of them than secular commanders? "Does it seem appropriate for a priest to be a soldier and a soldier a priest (*clericus miles—et miles clericus*)?" (LDO X, 16).

Her bold entry into the arena of public debate was so compelling and effective that she was soon spoken of as a voice to the nations, as a prophet for the times: "Who is this woman who rises out of the wilderness like a column of smoke from burning spices?" asked Pope Eugenius III, writing to commend her with an unusually metaphorical turn of phrase and supplying the answer to his own question: "You are the one who has become a life-enriching perfume for so many (*odor vitae in vitam*)" (Bw 33). Hildegard herself, however, never claimed to be the gifted visionary bringing light to those wandering aimlessly in the darkness that she certainly was for many of her admirers. She was, she said, "merely sounding a trumpet: a voice for the Voice that people might thus hear all the more clearly!"

It was in precisely this sense that she proclaimed the mysteries of creation: as the ways in which people related and were related to God and to his world, which were inseparably linked. There was only *one* reality. Human beings were living creatures in the midst of this real world, and at the end of their history they would live body and soul "in fully-realized harmony, solidarity, and unanimity."

Medieval people were well acquainted with this fundamental mystery of the world as an interconnected whole and made many interesting attempts to discover its implications. But no one among her contemporaries assessed the structure of the world and the nature of time as profoundly as Hildegard, the prophet of Rupertsberg near Bingen.

Medieval images

We still have access to a great variety of images of the medieval world: the illuminations and other works of art that present it in clear outlines and rich colours, gilded and even bejewelled. This is often how it springs before our mind's eye. The Middle Ages for the collector and historian of art can seem profoundly yet also misleadingly sumptuous. Even now, however, the world of the whole period remains largely mysterious, in spite of all the treasures we have available for its study, and, paradoxically, the more we learn of, say, its economic constraints, the impoverishment of the average human's everyday life, and the sufferings of sick people. But even if we try to keep to these particular aspects of the medieval experience of life and death, sickness and pain, crises and concerns, we discover that the only efficient way to understand them is to see them from the viewpoint of the world as a whole, which means in the perspective of its origin and destiny. Everything has to be seen in terms of one saving purpose.

In stone and colour, medieval art has preserved for us its conceptions of the world seen as a whole and presented in the dramatic imagery of the history of salvation: the Old Testament narratives of the creation of the world and its end, the making of the days that pass and of the plants and animals that enliven them. Angels as well as devils are alive for us though carved from stone, as are human beings—the whole person with his or her expectations, longings and fears, savagery, impulses, and tenderness—an essential element of the world seen whole and entire.

The Christian baptisteries grow out of the monuments of late antiquity and heathen tombs. The cross appears above classical sarcophagi, and the columned interiors of Roman temples are replaced by the naves of monastic churches. A whole world of the past is exorcised and reborn in the purifying flames of Christian enthusiasm. The old Adam dies and re-emerges into the light of a new life. The capitals in the interiors of churches are like pictorial chronicles—illustrated papers or magazines—hewn from stone. The pictures tell us about Adam and Eve, Abraham and Isaac, the Child in the crib and St Stephen, the Good Shepherd and the Good Samaritan, the City of God and the Last Judgement.

In stone, in murals, in manuscripts and on capitals we constantly encounter images of God the Father as the Creator of Eve from Adam's rib. Adam and Eve pluck grapes and get drunk. Abraham sees the Trinity and prays to the One God. Jonah is swallowed up in the whale's belly. Tobias heals his father's blindness. Jesus washes his disciples' feet, and Judas betrays the Lord with a kiss. The Good Shepherd goes in search of the lost sheep. The Prodigal Son returns home. The women grieve at the tomb of Jesus, and an angel comforts them.

It was such images of the Middle Ages that made it possible for the nineteenth-century mystical writer, Novalis, still to see them in these terms: "Those were glorious times when Europe was a single Christian country, when this region of the world shaped by human endeavours was the location of a single, undivided Christendom, and an all-encompassing common interest united even the outlying provinces of this far-flung spiritual realm."

"God's Justice" brings her accusation before the Supreme Judge:

Now I must call out and let my complaint resound. My crown has been tarnished by the schism caused by souls preaching error. No wonder, for each and every person wants to establish and follow the law of his or her own desires...! My robe is besmirched by the dust of the earth. Wanton people cover my garments in filth and never think of wiping themselves clean by doing penance. They have grown blind, deaf and dumb. They no longer sing God's praises. They no longer issue judgments that accord with my judgment. Instead they are entangled in the toils of avarice and never think of healing their wounds. All this has led to a wretched state of affairs in all the regular and fixed orders and degrees of the Church, causing it to proceed irresolutely, strutting at one moment and faltering at another, without staff or standard and with all its constitutions upset and uncertain. All degrees of the clerical estate are in darkness. All they want is to retain their titles without doing the work that justifies them. Accordingly, they have lost any possibility of true joy and happiness. But that is the result of what can only be called faith without works.

(Liber Divinorum Operum [Book of Divine Works] X, 11)

5. Eve
c. 1125;
Part of the door-lintel
from the north entrance
of Autun Cathedral

Religious life between tradition and reform

The medieval concept of order was one aspect of twelfth-century Europe that remained necessary and effective in spite of all the changes and turmoil. It was the ruling notion behind the *regula* of the religious Orders; and the *regula* was the framework of all their contributions to the work of salvation and, therefore, of all their efforts to heal what we would call breaches in the social fabric. The precise local origins and developing features of the various religious movements of the twelfth century were certainly inspired or affected by new ideas, but due order was essential to their beneficial progress. These and all other attempts at reform depended essentially on an underlying structure: the ideals and guidance of the gospel and the example of the Apostles.

New Orders had already been established in response to the Cluniac reform movement, the adaptation of the Rule of St Benedict initiated by Abbot Berno of Gigny (910) that radiated from the motherhouse at Cluny, near Mâcon in France. The Carthusians were founded in 1085, the Cistercians in 1098, and the Premonstratensians in 1120. The mendicant Orders—the Dominicans, Carmelites, Franciscans, and Augustinians—spread rapidly in the thirteenth century. Then there were loose groups such as the wandering preachers and other less orthodox tendencies all the way to the heretical Cathars and Waldensians. These also grew at considerable speed.

Since the attempt of the reforming Pope Gregory VII (1073-1085) to impose the spiritual over the temporal power there had been no halt to disputes about the division of power and rule. Yet the natural order seemed to call for the spiritual realm to remain in control of the means and instruments of salvation and of the ways of life and offices that applied them and through which they took effect. Accordingly and similarly, it was the duty of the secular realm to care for legal order and for the maintenance of peace. Although this remained the notional allocation of responsibilities, the Church's heavy burden of worldly possessions proved a constant source of contention and growing unrest.

The conflict between spiritual and secular interests continued throughout the twelfth century. Under the Emperor Frederick Barbarossa, however, the empire took on a quite novel "sacral" character; it was now the "*sacrum imperium*"—the Holy Empire. Henceforth this new conception was reinforced by the addition to the legal structure of the empire of an increasing number of features drawn from Roman law. It was not by chance that an anti-pope canonized Charlemagne at Barbarossa's behest and that, as a result, the Church consistently refused to confirm this elevation. Peace between Church and State was concluded only in 1177, in Venice. The Emperor, now absolved from excommunication, had to pay homage by prostrating himself before Pope Alexander, who nevertheless helped him up, gave him the kiss of peace, and blessed him.

Abbess Hildegard of Rupertsberg had been profoundly shocked by Barbarossa's attitude to the Pope and was not afraid to reprove her emperor. In a letter to him she said, "You may be King, but my mystical insight shows me very clearly that you are behaving like a child—even worse, in fact: like a fool! You just have to act with greater foresight. Take care that the Highest King of all doesn't throw you to the ground because of the blindness of your eyes, which are so ineffectual that you can't even see how to hold the sceptre in your hand and rule properly. Pull yourself together and start doing whatever is necessary to ensure that God's grace doesn't desert you altogether!" (Bw 86).

We can see that Hildegard was no indiffer-

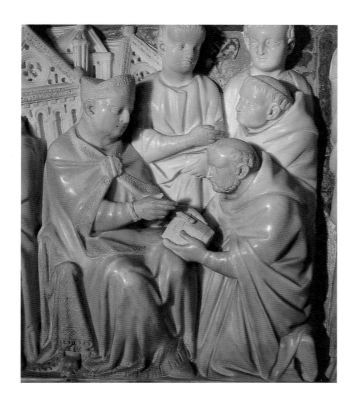

6. St Dominic submits the Rule of his Order to Pope Honorius III for Approval
Marble relief on Dominic's tomb in the church of S. Domenico in Bologna, carved by Niccolò Pisano, 1265/66

7. A Holy Ruler
c. 1200; probably a stained-glass window from the destroyed Romanesque cathedral in Strasbourg

21

ent or silent onlooker but felt that it was her duty to intervene in these disputes. As abbess and visionary she had to point out what others appeared not to see: that due justice was no longer exercised, either in the Church or in the empire. "This is what people will say to one another: How long do we have to tolerate and support these ravening wolves who are supposed to be physicians yet ignore their real vocation?" Consequently: "We are the victims of their crimes. The whole Church is rotting because they no longer preach truth and justice." They were robbers in charge of the Church's own holdings, seducers not teachers, and intent on corruption rather than instruction: "They use their sacred offices to impoverish us and put us in a state of real need, soiling not only themselves but us too in the process" (LDO X, 16).

Hildegard was against any kind of simony: "These evil people worm their way into the sacred building itself. By secret plotting, open theft, corrupt money, and the kind of maniacal fanaticism that stops at nothing, they manage to take over the offices ordained by God and carry on in this way until they have thrown the Church into turmoil and disorder" (Sc III, 9). She sent a solemn warning to Archbishop Hartwig of Bremen: "Beware! In these times the shepherds themselves are not only blind and lame, or busy robbing others of the money that brings death and destruction, but are actually intent on suppressing God's own justice!" (Bw 96). Even though God might allow "the rich to hold the wealth that they have stolen from the poor, he loves poor people more because they are his true image and likeness."

Heavenly values do not go with valuable possessions and large sums of money, Hildegard told Archbishop Arnold of Trier. What is more, she pointed out in the more gnomic, proverbial phraseology she sometimes used in her prophetic writings: "For this reason God deprives people of self-will so that they will learn how to long for their heavenly home. Accordingly, it is right that poor should love poor and rich vex rich. For wisdom gives a ring to the poor but denies earrings to the rich" (Bw 53). Here too Hildegard expressed her firm opposition to the practice of simony, which became increasingly shameless and outrageous in her lifetime. As she remarked in a letter to Archbishop Heinrich of Mainz:

"You should bewail and bemoan these times, shepherds of the Lord! Surely you are out of your minds when, just for the sake of cash, you squander divinely-established offices on evil people who use them for immoral ends!" (Bw 95).

But God simply would not permit "established offices (*officiales causae*) to be bought and sold with stolen money. People who do that are like poisonous scorpions. Deadly avarice courses so naturally through their veins that they not only greedily grab worldly titles and positions but creep into spiritual precincts in order to take them over too" (Sc III, 6).

It was in her popular preaching of the gospel message that Hildegard of Bingen most plainly expressed contemporary demands for a reformation of religious life. In the contentious borderline areas of religion and politics she undoubtedly said what she thought, but as prudently as the situation would allow. Where fundamental religious and moral issues were concerned, she spoke out fiercely and without compromise.

As a rule she highlighted and attacked the "womanish features of the present times," by which she meant the decadence of the Church; at best dubious, at worst sinister imperial policies; the obscuring and even suppression of spiritual truth by vague and erroneous doctrines and heresies; and especially the moral indifference and laxity of typical spiritual and temporal rulers. These were the main dangers. They were heightened by the threat of upheavals in religious life as a result of demands for revolutionary reforms from the laity and from the lower ranks of clergy, of new types of religious Order, and of changes in theology under the influence of increasingly rational approaches to philosophy.

Hildegard wrote to the Cologne clergy in prophetic mode: "Because you are so very wilful and change things without due attention to order, you are certain to experience violent disturbances in your own lifetime. They will confound you utterly" (Bw 172). She admonished the undisciplined monks of Hirsau as an "irresolute crew in a shipwrecked world," for: "The present onslaught by black and evil tyrants has unleashed on this world an age of injustice and of inglorious descent from the heights of glorious triumph" (Bw 133). She warned an abbot: "Look at the present sad plight of the so-called secluded monasteries as

8. **The Triple Wall of the Tower of the Church** *shows the way taken by the people of the Old Covenant to the Redeemer's Incarnation and God's plan of salvation in the Church, with accompany-* *ing figures representing the Virtues*
Liber Scivias, copy of the former Rupertsberg Codex, *c.* 1180; St Hildegard's Abbey, Eibingen

23

a result of totally ignoring the rule of obedience. That is why you suffer, and will suffer, so many ordeals" (Bw 181).

In the midst of all this unrest, however, the Benedictine way of life remained a source of reassurance. It is not too fanciful to say that the monasteries and their apparently unfailing adherence to the *ordo*, their particular expression of the idea of order, offered the Middle Ages a secure range of opportunities for healing and wholeness that fitted the vicissitudes of life. A monastery could still be *officina salutis et sanitatis* (a dispensary of salvation and health).

The monks scattered through forests and over heaths, in the wilds as it were, had become specialized scholars, and their mere centres of mendicancy had developed into the true schools of Europe. Yet the civilization of the western world was shaped not only by the formal and material circumstances of general education provided by the monasteries but, above all, by a moderate, decent, and cultured way of life and by a daily schedule that depended on ordered rhythms and deep spirituality. The instruments, outlines and tendencies of western culture were moulded by the reliable formality of everyday practice.

"O sweet breath of spring," said Bernard of Clairvaux in his refreshing commentary on the Song of Songs, "O summer enchantment, autumn fruitfulness and, not least of all, peace of mind in winter!" Life seemed constantly renewed even where death had left its mark, just as light fulfilled its promise and eventually broke through the gloomy watches of the night.

The appearance of all those breathtakingly beautiful Romanesque monasteries seemed to accord with this eternal process of rebirth and with the unerring movement of the seasons. The new edifices sprang from the earth (*surrexit domus*), as it were, as gracefully and naturally as the gazelle in the Song of Solomon, arching over the land and radiating their promise of illumination for the whole area roundabout. The very names of these holy places emphasized this clarity: Clairvaux ("Valley of Light"), Beaulieu ("Place of Beauty"), L'Escale-Dieu ("Divine Retreat"), and Claustrum Sancti Ruperti ("St Rupert's Cloister").

The *claustrum* was the characteristic form of this locus of divine radiance. It was an en-

closed clearing, carved out of the wild chaos of the surrounding forest land, and perfectly, indeed musically, attuned to an appropriate human rhythm. At the centre of this quadrilateral space was the human being, living in concord with the four natural elements, endowed with four humours, or essential psychophysical fluids, and aware of his or her accordance with the four cardinal points of the compass, the four seasons, and the four ages of cosmic history.

A "cloister" of this kind was a vast, complex yet perfectly phased clock-face with a mechanism that united within its walls all temporal rhythms, the cycles of years, months and days, and all the hours divided between action (*actio*) and contemplation (*contemplatio*). These Romanesque monasteries were indeed the natural realm in a quasi-human form, but entirely stripped down to essentials: the fixed skeletal structure together with the moving, integrated musculature that supported the sense and sensitivity of this functional as well as emblematic physicality. They were like crystalline summaries of the cosmos. The beauty of their stones still showed the marks of the work that had produced this quintessence and model of the whole. Everything was jointed, smoothed, fitted, and flexed to provide a versatile setting for the choral music that would resound there as the ages unfolded: the symphony of the New Jerusalem now evident on earth.

The gifts of God, Hildegard wrote, do not grow old like worn clothes. "They are always pure and simple, and therefore stay new for ever. They older they are, the more effective they become (*quando vetustiora tanto clariora*)" (Sc II, 5). But the world is still involved in a process of change and therefore of upheaval. "The sun of justice appeared to enlighten humanity and illumine human faith and action with good works, just as the dawn appears first and is followed by the hours of the day, until the light draws in and darkness begins to fall. In fact, my dear daughter, the world has changed in just that way," Hildegard wrote to her fellow-visionary, the younger Benedictine nun Elizabeth of Schönau. "It no longer possesses the same pulsating force that produced the virtues in all their original greenness. At times like this, however, God decides to give a new freshness to certain

9. St Elizabeth tends a
Sick Man in the
Convent—a place of
salvation as well as
healing (detail)

Cologne Master, late 14th
century;
Cologne, Wallraf-Richartz
Museum

25

people, so that his instruments do not run down but do their intended work efficiently" (Bw 196).

Hildegard saw herself as one of these divinely-chosen human instruments whom God had decided to enliven with a new, prophetic freshness and enthusiasm appropriate to the condition of the age.

The City of God on earth

A monastery was like a mighty city in miniature: an imitation of the *polis* of antiquity and also an image of the Heavenly Jerusalem. Unlike classical Greece and Rome, which developed for the most part as forms of urban culture, the monasteries were founded in country settings. These abbeys in peaceful rural environments evolved their own particular *regula*, or code of behaviour for leading a cultivated life, and thus became secluded domains of the intellect in the Christian West. They transmitted knowledge through their schools, scriptoria (or writing and illumination workshops), and libraries, and thus came to occupy a central position in the cultural landscape of Christian Europe.

Apart from the Benedictine way of life, it was mainly the reformed Orders and tendencies within Orders that were responsible for completely novel practices in the areas of economics and health or hygiene. They not only rationalized agriculture and forestry but established a planned form of biologically proficient nutrition and associated efficiently-conceived ways of caring for the poor and sick, together with a comprehensive approach to the care of the aged. Each monastery also soon possessed, as an integral part of its internal economy, an infirmary (*infirmarium*) and a herb garden (*hortus sanitatis*), usually accompanied by an apothecary's room, or pharmacy and perfumery (*armarium pigmentorum*). In addition to the sickroom for the use of the religious themselves there were hospices for the care of sick travellers (*hospitium*), together with special houses for the poor, sick, and pilgrims (*hospitale pauperum*). All these facilities composed the fixed institutions of the "compassionate work" (*misericordia*)

later made available to the needy in what came to be known as an "Hôtel-Dieu," or house of the guests of God.

There is every reason to suppose that in the generous planning and organization of the establishment on the Rupertsberg, Hildegard of Bingen explicitly followed the famous plan of the monastery of St Gallen (*c.* 830), with a physician's house, a pharmacy and a herb garden, baths and rooms for blood-letting in accordance with contemporary medical practice, a hospital, and numerous hygienic features. All this was supported by a surprisingly advanced form of economy for those times: land divided into plots for the cultivation of vegetables and vines, and then cattle-stalls and cellars, as well as a mill and a brewery, a smithy, workshops, and the fish-pond that to modern eyes often seems a rather charming adjunct to the other elements. New methods of agriculture and novel craft techniques meant that the religious Orders were a primary factor of European economic life as a whole, quite apart from the effects of, say, their sanitary measures and organized approaches to health.

The intellectual renewal of these religious communities that had begun in the eleventh century was closely associated with an economic upturn evident not only in the care of the poor and sick but in social welfare facilities and in artistic activities. In the eleventh and twelfth centuries the Cluniacs in particular were responsible for a vigorous renewal and development of architecture and building in France, northern Italy, Flanders, Lorraine, and Germany. This movement produced the great monasteries such as Cluny itself or Hirsau but also cathedrals as in Tournai or Speyer. They were far too big for the needs of the population then, but still too small, as far as their designers and builders were concerned, to show forth the majesty of God.

The monastery became a matrix for cultivating and civilizing everyday life, so that the contemplative way remained influential in spite of all the surrounding agitation of secular society.

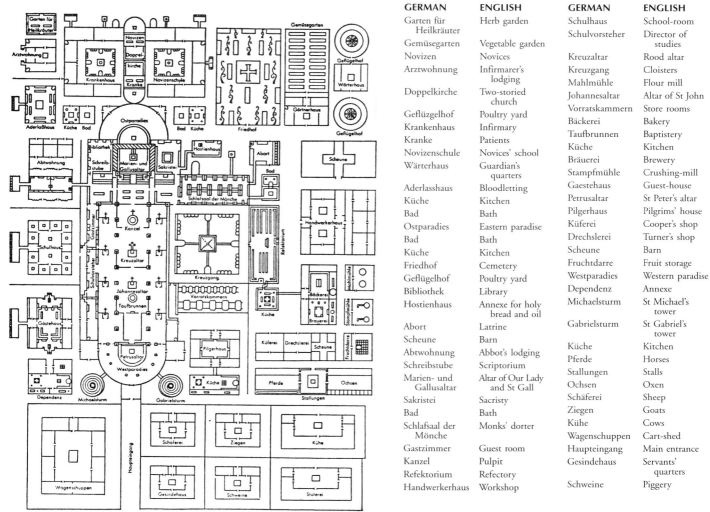

GERMAN	ENGLISH	GERMAN	ENGLISH
Garten für Heilkräuter	Herb garden	Schulhaus	School-room
Gemüsegarten	Vegetable garden	Schulvorsteher	Director of studies
Novizen	Novices	Kreuzaltar	Rood altar
Arztwohnung	Infirmarer's lodging	Kreuzgang	Cloisters
Doppelkirche	Two-storied church	Mahlmühle	Flour mill
Geflüzgelhof	Poultry yard	Johannesaltar	Altar of St John
Krankenhaus	Infirmary	Vorratskammern	Store rooms
Kranke	Patients	Bäckerei	Bakery
Novizenschule	Novices' school	Taufbrunnen	Baptistery
Wärterhaus	Guardian's quarters	Küche	Kitchen
Aderlasshaus	Bloodletting	Bräuerei	Brewery
Küche	Kitchen	Stampfmühle	Crushing-mill
Bad	Bath	Gaestehaus	Guest-house
Ostparadies	Eastern paradise	Petrusaltar	St Peter's altar
Bad	Bath	Pilgerhaus	Pilgrims' house
Küche	Kitchen	Küferei	Cooper's shop
Friedhof	Cemetery	Drechslerei	Turner's shop
Geflügelhof	Poultry yard	Scheune	Barn
Bibliothek	Library	Fruchtdarre	Fruit storage
Hostienhaus	Annexe for holy bread and oil	Westparadies	Western paradise
		Dependenz	Annexe
Abort	Latrine	Michaelsturm	St Michael's tower
Scheune	Barn	Gabrielsturm	St Gabriel's tower
Abtwohnung	Abbot's lodging		
Schreibstube	Scriptorium	Küche	Kitchen
Marien- und Gallusaltar	Altar of Our Lady and St Gall	Pferde	Horses
		Stallungen	Stalls
Sakristei	Sacristy	Ochsen	Oxen
Bad	Bath	Schäferei	Sheep
Schlafsaal der Mönche	Monks' dorter	Ziegen	Goats
		Kühe	Cows
Gastzimmer	Guest room	Wagenschuppen	Cart-shed
Kanzel	Pulpit	Haupteingang	Main entrance
Refektorium	Refectory	Gesindehaus	Servants' quarters
Handwerkerhaus	Workshop		
		Schweine	Piggery

10. **Plan of St Gallen Monastery c. 830;**
reconstructed drawing
The original plan, which has survived, is studied in great detail by Walter Horn and Ernest Born, The Plan of St Gall, *3 vols., Univ. of California Press (1979).*

11. **Reconstruction of the Layout of Cluny Monastery c. 1150**
reconstructed drawing
by K. J. Conant

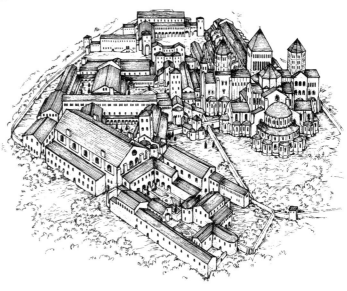

If we want to escape the torments of hell and obtain everlasting life, while we still have the opportunity, are in this world, and can do all this in the circumstances of our life now, we must waste no more time but immediately start behaving in a way that will benefit us for all eternity. To ensure this we intend to found a school for the Lord's service. We hope to establish nothing crude or oppressive in this institution. Nevertheless, you may find this or that aspect of it rather rigorous, even though it has actually been decided quite fairly in order to correct our evil inclinations and to safeguard the rule of love. If you do find this way of life hard, do not give in to transient anxieties or desert the way of salvation, which is always difficult to start with. In fact, as you progress in the religious life and in faith, you will find your heart widening until it almost bursts with the indescribably sweet fullness of love, and you are able to run along the path of God's commandments. Knowing this, we shall never abandon his teaching but practise his doctrine until we die. We shall persevere in the monastery, share patiently in the sufferings of Christ, and thus deserve to be granted a place in his kingdom. Amen.

(Conclusion of the Prologue to the Rule of St Benedict)

12. St Benedict
Benevento, 11th century;
Rome, Vatican Library

Scenery of an exceptional life

The Bermersheim estate

The village of Bermersheim is located in the Nahegau district of Rheinhessen, not far from Alzey Castle. The official records of the imperial abbey of Lorsch testify to its existence as early as 769 to 797. On the way out of the village, you would have come to the family estate of the freeborn nobility of Bermersheim, of Rhenish-Franconian stock.

The basic supportive structure of a small community of this kind was the "house" or "home," more properly the "household," to which the term "family" was applied only in later centuries. The early medieval family was primarily an ethnically homogeneous community and therefore also a "lineage," or branch of a clan or tribe (though kinship terminology is a highly contentious field and there are as many definitions as there are theorists). It was only in the thirteenth century that the family name became a descriptive term of major significance alongside a person's Christian name. The household was a form of legal union, a common dwelling-place and property, and a joint centre of general and domestic economy (*oeconomia*).

"Usage" became an increasingly dominant factor, regulating mutual consent and standards of behaviour, but "wisdom" was also an effective basis of all legal rules and directives in a household. All those living there shared in the communal process of production and consumption. The head of the household provided for the care and welfare of all those entrusted to him, of whom, therefore, he was "in charge." A "family" of this kind was a community that offered its members all the necessary procedures of life and development, from which they benefited as law, usage, and wisdom dictated. Accordingly it was also an educational community and one that handed on its inheritance. This meant not only immovable property, goods and chattels, but

tradition and honour. It offered protection from poverty and need and to do this had to shape its own particular forms and ways of living and coping with the demands of existence. The medieval kin-group in the foregoing sense was the basis from which that smaller civil entity, the family in the more modern sense, eventually developed.

The head of the household, the "father," exercised wisdom and foresight by determining the norms that applied in the group and by according each member what he or she needed and deserved. He would intervene duly and monitor and control everything with propriety and discipline and in due measure. A community of this kind was the setting in which each human being became acquainted with the reality of fatherliness and motherliness and learned what it meant to be a child, which meant the son or daughter of a father and a mother in a home of this kind. It afforded one of the fundamental patterns of human existence for emotional formation, education, socialization, religious experience, and their internalization by each individual. We must bear all this in mind when considering the implications for Hildegard of terms such as "father," "mother," "love" and so on in various written contexts.

In 1098 Hildegard was born into a *familia* of this kind as the tenth child of the noble Hildebert, who still gave his name as Vermers in a deed dated 1127. His daughter was probably christened in the little church attached to the estate.

The Bermersheim clan undoubtedly belonged to the high nobility, and Hildegard, who became the *magistra* ("leader" or "ruler") of her community, always remained aware of her elevated status. Her nephew Arnold, archbishop of Trier, was one of the foremost princes of the Church in the empire. Conrad,

13. The Church where Hildegard was baptized

Count Palatine, who was Barbarossa's step-brother, granted special privileges to her abbey at Rupertsberg. Hildegard exercised the relations allowed her by rank and status with the Margrave of Stade and the Count Palatine of Stahleck. She was on friendly terms with Countess Bertha, sister of King Conrad III and wife to Hermann of Stahleck.

We know very little about the early years of Hildegard's childhood. Nevertheless the names of seven of her nine brothers and sisters have come down to us. Drutwin, the eldest brother, is named together with his father as a witness in a deed of 1127. Hugo held the office of precentor or choirmaster of Mainz Cathedral. Roricus was a canon at Tholey in the Saar. Four sisters are mentioned: Irmengard, Odilia, Jutta, and Clementia, who later became a nun in Hildegard's convent.

Hildegard's biographer tells us only that her parents Hildebert and Mechtild took their clever daughter in 1106 to the Benedictine cloister of Disibodenberg, and put her in the charge of the recluse Jutta von Spanheim, who had established the community of anchoresses there. As the tenth child, Hildegard was presumably dedicated to God and now became *inclusa*, "enclosed." Henceforth she was to be educated and "formed" in seclusion from the "world," which for some years was virtually mediated to her through Jutta, her only guide and real human contact. When she was sixteen she received the habit of a Benedictine nun from Bishop Otto of Bamberg in the same convent.

Hildegard had shown signs of exceptional intuition and intelligence from her earliest years. "The Lord hath called me from the womb," she wrote, citing the prophet Isaiah (49: 1). "From the bowels of my mother hath he made mention of my name." As she put it in her own words: "God imprinted this visionary power (*visio*) on me from the moment I was formed (*prima formatione*), when he breathed life into me and called me into existence in my mother's womb (*in utero matris*)!" (V II, 2).

The same faculty of vision and insight accompanied Hildegard throughout her life.

Disibodenberg Monastery

The origins of the cloister at Disibodenberg date back to the early Middle Ages. Around 700 the Irish monk Disibodus went to Germany and withdrew to a "wild and lonely area" at the mouth of the river Glan in the Nahe region. There he founded a monastery in conformity with the Rule of St Benedict. The monastery prospered particularly between 1108 and 1143 under Stephan von Spanheim, the father of the *magistra* Jutta who took charge of Hildegard's education. 1108 also saw the start of a long period of building on to the monastery and of considerable extension and change for the church and community. Archbishop Heinrich I of Mainz solemnly dedicated the new basilica in 1143.

Hildegard became *magistra* of the women's community in 1136. Throughout the years of construction and expansion she must have observed and learned many of the implications of all the building activities and of such things as the development of scholarly links with neighbouring convents. The relations with Trier and its monasteries and archbishops were particularly close. It was at Trier that Pope Eugenius III with a great retinue held a synod from November 1147 to mid-February 1148 and in the course of it tested and eventually confirmed the "visions" of the nun Hildegard. For Hildegard, Trier was not only the starting-point of her many and many-sided contacts with important people in the empire and Church but a focus for her own activities. A few years after the Trier synod she had already established her own convent at Rupertsberg. The foundation was followed by the creation of productive links between her community and the convents of St Eucharius, St Matthias, and St Maximin.

These activities alone were certainly exceptional for any medieval woman. To them Hildegard added the many exhausting duties of the director of a community of nuns. She was also responsible for the complex administrative functions that became necessary as the concept and nature of a group of dedicated holy women with so many areas of interest were developed and expanded. Soon, a quite separate convent, independent of the monastery, had to be founded to ensure that all these functions and departments were duly integrated into a regular pattern of life yet evolved with full respect for each specialism.

The Rupertsberg Convent

The foundation of a separate convent did not proceed without objections from the monks at Disibodenberg. The external pressures on Hildegard were also immense. Nevertheless, in 1152 Archbishop Heinrich of Mainz consecrated a convent chapel for the new foundation. He also presented the community with the "Mühlenwerth," a "mill site" on Lake Bingen.

Hildegard had acquired the site for building her convent by buying land from Hermann, dean of Mainz, and from Count Bernhard of Hildesheim. In addition there were various gifts and also the dues in kind and rents from several estates or farms. The most important acquisition was Bermersheim, a legacy that Hildegard's brothers and sisters assigned to the abbey of Rupertsberg. Constant donations and exchanges, purchases and bequests made the convent a very valuable land-owning entity that needed effective legal protection.

The convent received due confirmation in accordance with canon law with the granting of two deeds, or charters, that Archbishop Arnold of Mainz ordered to be drawn up on 22 May 1158. We know the names of a number of illustrious witnesses to these deeds, such as the abbots of St Alban and Jac in Mainz, Abbot Helingar of Disibodenberg, Abbot Anselm of Johannesberg in the Rheingau, the deans of Mainz and Frankfurt, and Counts Gottfried of Sponheim, Konrad of Kirchberg, Emicho of Bamberg and Berthold of Nidda.

On 14 April 1163 the imperial edict of protection was read out at a royal audience in Mainz. In future, anyone attempting to take the cloister under his jurisdiction would come under the threat of punishment by imperial justice (*imperiali dextera*).

The eminent witnesses named in Barbarossa's edict of "safe-conduct" constitute an exceptional testimony not only to the extent of Hildegard's activity at the time but to public interest in the visionary's work. The first witness was one of the greatest princes of the Church of his time: Conrad of Wittelsbach, brother of Otto of Wittelsbach, duke of Bavaria. Conrad was archbishop of Mainz from 1161 to 1165 and from 1183 to 1200. Hildegard had written to him and advised him affectionately to receive in his heart the "beautiful rays of divine justice," to be kept there like a "tender and enchanting female companion in your bosom" (Bw 48). The next witness in the deed was Archbishop Wigmann of Magdeburg.

Then there were Eberhard of Biburg and Hipelstein, who was Archbishop of Salzburg from 1143 to 1164. Hildegard had tried to show this powerful prince of the Church, who made repeated attempts to mediate between the emperor and the pope, that both aspiration to the heavenly kingdom and care for the

---

Finally God's servant and eighteen consecrated virgins moved from the place where she had remained until then. Though her departure was most painful and sad for those whom she left behind, she brought great joy and pleasure to the site where she now settled. For many eminent persons and a considerable crowd of ordinary people, exulting with holy songs, came out from the town of Bingen and the places roundabout to greet and receive her. When Hildegard and her little band had occupied the place prepared for them, with a pious and joyful heart she praised the divine wisdom that runs through all things, embraced with motherly love the nuns entrusted to her care, and never ceased instructing them skilfully in the Rule of their community. In order to avoid any impression of crudely taking over or confiscating others' possessions, she acquired the site where she now resided from its former owners with the aid of gifts from the faithful, partly by paying for it, and partly by barter. Since she had obtained it freely, she determined that it would always remain free. It would be subject only to the protection of the church of Mainz, and have no defender other than the archbishop of that see. It was important to ensure that no one thought she might accept a secular overlord, and thereby let a wolf into the byre where the sheep lay, though very many churches on this earth suffer from such abuses and are destroyed by them.

(*Hildegardis Vita* [The Life of Hildegard], I, 7).

people could be combined in a "*single* form of service" (Bw 73). The next witness after him was Archbishop Heinrich of Würzburg.

His was followed by yet another prominent name, that of the influential Archbishop Eberhard of Bamberg (1146-1170), who had left the imperial audience in Mainz in 1163 to visit Hildegard on the Rupertsberg. She had sent him a long letter in which she tried to show him how authentic values depended on good works (Bw 71). A further witness was Archbishop Hartmann of Brixen. He was followed by Bishop Henry of Liège (1145-1164), who had often accompanied Frederick Barbarossa when he gave royal audiences, but also on imperial campaigns. Hildegard had complained to this Bishop Henry about the dire condition of the times, with particular reference to unworthy shepherds from whom no good things flowed but only justifiable discontent and lamentation (Bw 65).

The next witness in the document is Bishop Gottfried of Utrecht (1156-1177), who was chosen for his office in the presence of Barbarossa. He also appeared at Frederick's audience in Mainz in April 1163. The next major witness after him was a secular authority, Conrad, Count Palatine of the Rhine and step-brother to Barbarossa. In the same year (1163) he granted the Rupertsberg community special privileges for the conventual possessions in the Palatinate. Then there was Duke Henry of Bavaria and Saxony, followed by a company of other noble witnesses.

In 1171 Archbishop Christian of Mainz also extended tax concessions to the convent by a grant of privilege. In 1187 Archbishop Conrad of Mainz confirmed its legal status and once again placed the convent under the protection of the Mainz episcopal authorities.

Eibingen Convent

In 1165 Hildegard acquired and occupied the by then deserted Augustinian cloister in Eibingen above Rüdesheim, which had been founded by the nobleman Marka of Rüdesheim. Twice a week the abbess crossed the Rhine at Nachen to visit her daughter house, where she had restored the ruined buildings to accommodate thirty Benedictine nuns. She continued to supervise the new house until late in her life. In 1636, after the destruction of their convent by Swedish troops during the Thirty Years' War, the Rupertsberg nuns took Hildegard's relics and went by way of Cologne to settle in Eibingen.

The Eibingen convent had an eventful history. It was closed down in 1802 and refounded only a century later. The new convent was constructed between 1900 and 1904, though no longer on the original site in Eibingen itself, but high up above, in the middle of the Weinberg hills and surrounded by an extensive garden area. On 17 September 1904 the convent was occupied by nuns from the Benedictine abbey of St Gabriel in Prague. The new conventual church was consecrated on 7 September 1908.

This convent too was permeated by the Hildegardian spirit, which the monk Guibert of Gembloux praised in a letter of report to his brothers: "Here everything breathes prayerful devotion, holiness and peace. On Sundays the spinning wheels, spindles, and quill-pens are at rest. Pious reading and liturgical singing take place in an atmosphere of sacred silence. But on weekdays they fulfil the words of the Apostle: 'Whoever does not work, shall not eat!'" (Pi 406).

In all these places Hildegard offered the people of her own times a practical demonstration of one of her central themes: God's generosity in offering the world so many gifts, both actual and potential. God had certainly given people the faculty of reason, but so that they could work creatively in many different ways. This notion was the basis of Hildegard's profound experience and expression of her joy in and about existence. It was also the foundation of her essentially sensuous reception and perception of so many aspects of the world and life (*constitutio*). It also lay behind her sensitivity to and existential sympathy with all forms of suffering (*destitutio*). This sense of oneness with the cosmos enabled her to recognize and depict the longing and striving of all creation for redemption (*restitutio*). For Hildegard, one and the same spirit constantly refreshes the whole world, infusing its greenness into all things until they ripen to the point of visible fruition. Life, our life, becomes palpable reality by virtue of the light that shines through and from the natural world. All forms of nature are one.

Hildegard's unusually varied natural abilities were coupled with good fortune. Her upbringing favoured their development. Her personal-

*15. Rupertsberg Convent
before its Destruction in
the Thirty Years' War*
Engraving *c.* 1620

*16. St Hildegard's Abbey,
Eibingen*

ity was cultivated to just the degree that allowed her to respond to the possibilities of all these locations and opportunities and to mature effectively. Her childhood piety went hand-in-hand with the familiarity with nature and sensitivity to it of someone brought up on the land. Her Benedictine discretion fitted her aristocratic reserve, and her poetic sensibility was the perfect accompaniment to her profound conviction of ultimate purpose and to her sense of mission. But heredity and environment do not wholly explain the nature and achievements of her years of development. The additional factors were Hildegard's receptivity but also her questioning; her willingness to listen but also her drive to perceive; her readiness to respond but also her impulse to understand. She undoubtedly had pious inclinations, but what made them so unusually productive was her essentially investigative and questing spirit. She was quite aware of this and constantly stressed its importance: "If human beings ask no questions, the Holy Spirit gives no answers."

Everyday life in Hildegard's convent

When he saw the Rupertsberg Convent (so the monk Guibert of Gembloux wrote to tell his friend Bodo in the second half of 1177), he thought he had been magically transported to the fabled Land of Milk and Honey. He gave a detailed account of this paradise:

"There you can observe all the virtues marvellously competing to outdo one another. The mother receives her daughters with such great love, and the daughters submit to their mother with such immense respect, that it is scarcely possible to decide whether the mother exceeds the daughters, or the daughters the mother in enthusiasm. These holy servants care for one another and in this way honour and respect one another, so that with Christ's help, though they are members of the weaker sex, they make glad display of their triumph over themselves, the world and the devil. On feastdays they sit becomingly in their seclusion and consecrate themselves zealously to reading and to learning the skills of holy singing. And they heed the words of the Apostle: 'If you do not labour you shall not eat.'"

Guibert continues his description with details of other remarkable features of the Rupertsberg convent that bring to life the everyday practice of a medieval community of nuns: "On working days they are busy in their respective workshops or writing books, making liturgical vestments, and carrying out other handiwork. Their assiduous reading affords them divine illumination and the grace of contrition, whereas the accomplishment of their outward labours wards off indolence, the enemy of the soul, and suppresses talkativeness, an inclination that in idle and frivolous company only too easily forces far too many words from human mouths."

Within a few years, Guibert says, this convent had been able to develop to such an extent that its impressive buildings offered space and support for fifty nuns and for staff and guests, so effectively indeed that all the workshops were equipped with pipes for running water.

But the "marvel" that the monk from Flanders found especially appealing was that: "This convent was founded not by an emperor or bishop, not by any of the rich and mighty people of this earth, but by a poor and tender woman." Finally, Guibert comes to the underlying attitude and spirit that this mere woman Hildegard was able to impart to her community: "But the mother and leader of this great company devotes herself to them all in the spirit of love. With the vast weight of her modesty she overwhelms the threat of arrogance that generally springs from outward renown. In this way, through sheer love and devotion she has become the servant of all. She is always responsive to whatever demands the moment makes upon her, to everyday needs and requirements. She gives advice, solves difficult problems, writes books, instructs her sisters, and encourages sinners in their struggles when they approach her with their worries. However age and sickness afflict her, she remains strong in the exercise of all the virtues and has made many apostolic recommendations her very own watchwords; for example: 'I have become all for all in order to win all'; or: 'I may be inexperienced in speaking but not in knowledge'; or: 'Most gladly therefore will I rather glory in my infirmities, that the power of Christ may rest upon me'; and more of the same kind."

Guibert also told Bodo and his astonished brothers in Flanders how on feastdays Hildegard's nuns stood round the altar of the conventual church, their hair flowing and adorned with radiant white veils as they sang their holy songs. They also wore golden tiaras or circlets on their heads, with roundels bearing the sign of the cross and the image of the Lamb. Their hands were decorated with golden rings ornamented with jewels. They not only sang radiantly but seemed to float rather than merely move along the corridors of the convent, chanting: "*O virga ac diadema!*" —"Hail, Mary, branch of David's line! Hail, Virgin clad in purple royal! Hail, Mary, crown of David's tree!"

17. Hildegard the
visionary and prophetess
recording what she had
seen (detail)
Liber Divinorum
Operum, *c.* 1240; Ms
1942, Lucca, Biblioteca
Statale

36

2. A woman's life

muſicoꝝ · De ſimpﬁonia ĩ laudib̃ ·
s. marie & cuuũ ſupnoꝝ gaudioꝝ
et omniũ ſcoꝝ ·

*18. **Hildegard of Bingen
on her Balcony** (detail)*
Salem Scivias Codex,
13th century,
Cod. Sal. X 16, fol. 3v
Heidelberg, University
Library

38

Stages in life

Hildegard was a little girl at home until she was eight. She experienced the first years of childhood among her brothers and sisters on her father's estate at Bermersheim. We would know very little about that time if Hildegard herself had not given us a quite remarkable account of it. Even in infancy—so she tells us later—she became aware that she possessed a strange intuitive understanding that affected her while awake and seemed to come upon her with extraordinary intensity. At various times she referred to this unusual experience as her "perception," "visionary insight," "illumination," or "reflection of the living Light." She tried to explain these "marvellous secret visions" to a few others but soon realized that people around her not only saw nothing like that but had no idea what she was talking about.

Hildegard described her experiences as follows: "At first, if my visionary insight seized me and flowed through me with all its power, I would speak out and start telling people one thing after the other that I had seen, but they soon made it quite obvious that they found my behaviour very odd indeed. This made me ashamed of what was happening to me. I used to cry a lot and reached the point where I desperately wanted to say absolutely nothing about it all. But, somehow, that just wasn't possible. All the same, I was so afraid of other people's reactions that, although I couldn't stop myself saying that I saw things, I took care to say nothing about *how* I saw them" (V II, 16).

As she grew up her "inner vision" became even more intense and emphatic and the imagery more precise, especially when the young Hildegard was put under the care of the anchoress Jutta von Spanheim at the Disibodenberg monastery. "The only person I told about this was Jutta, the well-born woman who had been put in charge of my

education" (V II, 16). It was then that a mysterious inner voice began to speak to her about the real meaning of her visions: "Poor creature! You are the daughter of many pains, and physically parched and withered as a result of the severe ill-health your body has so often suffered from. In spite of all this, you have been plunged into the depths of God's own mysteries. So never forget but record what you have seen with your inner eye and heard with the ear of your soul!"

Hildegard paid increasing attention to the inner voice and its commands: "Write down what you see and tell people what you hear!" Finally the rather worried, in fact scared, nun decided to tell Abbot Kuno of Disibodenberg about these visions. He said he thought the most sensible thing was to write them all down. Then they would be able to judge the outcome and decide what it meant. Hildegard's inward disquiet had also made her turn to the great Abbot Bernard of Clairvaux for help. She wrote to him about her physical and mental experiences and troubles and confided in the already famous churchman (whom, of course, she had never met in reality but only in visions): "I am wretched, indeed more than wretched as the woman I am, but even in early childhood I saw great, even miraculous things. Yet ever since I was an infant I have never known peace for a single hour." Utterly depressed by the unremitting "descent of the beam in the wine-press" of her nature, she begged Bernard for comfort, help and advice: "But I just have to write to you, because you are always able to lift the beam and emerge triumphant in the spiritual struggle. I need the advice of someone who can raise himself, and the world along with him, ever upward to salvation" (Bw 25/26).

Bernard's reply was very careful and duly reticent. He reminded his visionary correspondent that she was obviously the only one in a position to know exactly how she experienced these things. Consequently she herself was the best judge of what to say and do about them. Eventually, when the synod opened at Trier in 1147, Archbishop Henry of Mainz gave an account of Hildegard and her visions to Pope Eugenius III. The Pope was obviously captivated by the description, for he decided to send a commission under Archbishop Albero of Verdun to the Disibodenberg convent itself to carry out a full critical investigation of the phenomena and to decide exactly what was going on. The results were entirely favourable, so much so that the Pope himself was impressed enough to organize a reading from Hildegard's writings before the assembled dignitaries of the Church. In this way he officially confirmed the quality of her gifts and encouraged her to make a written record of her visions.

Now the years of patient waiting, puzzlement, and physical suffering were over. Hildegard embarked on and completed her first major written work: "Know the Ways of the Lord" (*Sci vias Domini*).

Later *Magistra Hildegardis* wrote to a *magister*, or male leader and counsellor, in Paris to bewail her physical weakness and acknowledge her lack of a classical education of the kind then available to men: "I am not brimming with human knowledge and scholarship. I am not gifted with a particularly outstanding intellect. I have to rely entirely on God's help." She saw herself as a wholly insignificant little feather that the Lord of all glories had decided to raise from the ground, spinning it into movement on the currents of his own divine wind, which "blows where it will." Yes, she knew that she was a visionary and a prophetess, but what she saw and uttered came from the very heights and depths of God. Thus illuminated and enlightened, as prophets must be, she would write in obedience to that compulsion. She would write precisely and straightforwardly, holding nothing back of what had been vouchsafed her to transmit to others. She knew that her response to God's action on her was not scholarship or theology, or anything like the usual form of human inquiry in accordance with the conventions of an ecclesiastical training at that time. It was nothing less than direct illumination by the power of the living God: "… the living light of the Holy Spirit in the mysterious Word issuing from the wisdom of the Father."

The literary works

The many accounts of Hildegard that have come down to us unmistakably reveal her ability to listen to her inner voice and to transcribe its meaning; her originality, in other words. Her charismatic gifts were recognized by the highest authority in the Church, which not only permitted but enjoined her to proclaim the vision that she thereby heeded as it deserved. From then on, always inquiring into and admiring the true glory of the world and the outward beauty and inward vitality of our physical existence, she found the right means of expression for what is best described as a truly loving heart.

For ten years, from 1141 to 1151, Hildegard worked on her *Liber Scivias*: a unique interfusion of cosmology, anthropology, and theology. Its twenty-six visions describe the creation of the world, the fall of the angels, the creation and fall of humanity, and the "ardent labour of redemption" carried out by Christ and his Church. She depicts the mystery of salvation as the construction of a vast edifice through expanses of space and aeons of time until the Last Judgment, the day of the final and great revelation at the end of the ages.

Between 1158 and 1163 she wrote the *Liber Vitae Meritorum*, a practical guide to living, with dramatic exchanges between the vices and virtues. The scenery here is drawn from the events and conflicts of daily life, but the essence of the work is the intimate interaction between humanity and the cosmos, the cooperative nature of creation, and the ways in which it "looks to its Creator as the beloved to her Lover."

Hildegard recorded the cosmic visions of the *Liber Divinorum Operum* in the decade from 1163 to 1173. The "Book of Divine Works" is rightly seen as her main creative achievement. In ten visions she unfolds the history of salvation from Genesis to the Apocalypse and its cosmological infrastructure. She sees the order of creation as encompassing not only, say, the angelic world but the kingdom of plants and animals. She demonstrates the connections between the life of the senses and the workings of grace and locates human beings, the body and soul, world and Church,

19. **Hildegard**

In the preface to "Know the Ways" (Scivias), the Rupertsberg Codex shows Hildegard the visionary sitting in her cell, flanked by pillars representing the Old and New Covenants. The five-tongued beam of divine inspiration pierces through the roof and encloses the prophetess' head. She supports a wax tablet on her knee with one hand, and holds a stylus in the other as she prepares to describe what she sees and hears. The monk Volmar watches her intently, ready to help her record her visionary experience.

Liber Scivias, copy of the former
Rupertsberg Codex,
c. 1180;
St Hildegard's Abbey,
Eibingen

nature and grace in a single economy of responsibility: in one indivisible reality.

For Hildegard, God himself appears to us as love in this world and has placed love within all of us as our principle of order. Love is the essential setting of all purpose and direction in life. As she wrote to Bishop Eberhard II of Bamberg: "The Father of us all is illumination, and illumination is both radiance and fire, clarity and inspiration, which are one and the same light. If you do not understand this in faith you do not see God for what he is, because you are trying to separate him from what he really is, and God is one: he cannot be divided. Even the works made by God lose their original meaning when human beings divide them up. This illumination is our Father's love, by which all things come into being and which surrounds all things, for all that is depends on the power of love." And: "Love is a fire that can never be put out. It is the vital source of the flames of true faith enlightening the hearts of real believers. Love of God sets them on fire with a faith they could never enjoy if they did not already love him in their hearts." The old Abbess Hildegard wrote these beautiful words to her restless young admirer, Guibert of Gembloux, and closed her letter thus: "This means that the order of love (ordinatio caritatis) sustains you too, Guibert" (Pi 400).

It is difficult to know what aspect of this work most deserves praise: its refined spiritual structure; the rhythmic development of its drama; the depth of the faith evident throughout; its compelling ardour; or the beauty of its language and the imagery of its mystical visions.

Only repeated readings of the text enable us to discover its special lyricism. This tender poetry has a strange beauty that gradually seizes us in the rhythm of the sentences, in the profound and echoing meaning upon meaning of the metaphors, in the flow and pattern of symbols and leitmotifs building toward a supreme allegory, in the definition of the imagery, in the tonality of its colours, and in Hildegard's ability to make us experience worlds and scenes as a harmonious setting in which we too begin to move effortlessly. At the same time, anyone familiar with other medieval texts must notice the almost total absence of conventional tropes and tricks of scholastic rhetoric. This can makes her style seem rather wooden and sometimes rough in comparison, but it is to Hildegard's advantage that she was not trained in ways that might have made her works slick but unoriginal. At times certain long, dull, and rather dutiful passages tend to obscure the full delight of her imagery, but the power of her inspiration always breaks through and gathers force until breathtaking sublimity redeems the now forgotten tedium.

Visual artistry

Hildegard's visual creations are closely connected with her literary work. She is one of that select company of writers who were also impressively gifted as visual artists. In one sense, this is not so strange an accomplishment for those whose natural ability is lyrical rather than technical, imaginative rather than discursive. Yet there is a strong architectonic element in Hildegard's creative work in literature, art, and music. God himself is known as the summus artifex, the highest of all architects, and Hildegard's work is richly seeded with the imagery of building and construction: Noah's Ark, the Tower of Babel, the Heavenly Jerusalem are central images for her. One of her key-words and main concepts is aedificare = constructing or building. The Church is praised as the edifice of salvation (aedificatio salutis); and the enlightened creation appears as the Golden City (civitas aurea). It is surely no accident that in the group of paintings that make up his great Isenheim Altar at Colmar, in Alsace, Matthias Grünewald placed Hildegard's convent in a central position, seemingly hovering between Heaven and Earth.

Hildegard presents God as the great creative master-hand, a profoundly expert artist, a virtuous chief builder and architect, a careful gardener, a marvellous smith and metalworker. This was in the biblical tradition that portrayed God as weaver and embroiderer, potter and designer, architect and artist. "God acts like a skilled craftsman (operarius) who tests his glowing workpiece under the bellows, rehandling, turning and remaking his handiwork until it is quite perfect" (LVM IV, 68). Similarly, "every day, as they proceed on their way to salvation, human beings use their skill and craft to pare off and abandon everything unprofitable, whether they are looking or hearing, smelling, tasting, or touching, like

20./21. Centre Panel of the Isenheim Altarpiece, first side, detail
Matthias Grünewald
(1512-16)
Colmar, Unterlinden
Museum.

43

*22. **God the Father calculating the Dimensions of the World***
Didactic Bible, mid-13th century
Cod. 2554. Fol. 1r
Vienna, Austrian National Library

artists who spend a great deal of time scraping, shaping, and rehandling their works until they finally stand there in all the beauty of due and proper form" (Pi 44).

Elsewhere Hildegard compares God's construction of the world to a master gardener laying out his work: "A master who wants to design a garden most proficiently first of all finds a suitable site. Then, if he wants to be both a great philosopher (*magnus philosophus*) and an expert craftsman (*profundus artifex*), he finds the right place for each variety, and considers the fruitfulness and utility of different kinds of trees and vegetables, chooses the really good ones, and plants them. Then he erects a protective wall around his garden and appoints an under gardener who knows how to water the site, collect the fruits of the various plants, and make different remedies (*pigmenta*) from them" (Sc I, 2).

God the supreme artist has also fashioned and continually refashions his special creation, human beings, whom he never deserts. He is *Deus faber*, God the Maker, who appoints humans as his apprentices and co-workers and hands them the designs and guidelines for their tasks. Just as God in his creative power (*virtus fortitudinis*) is the "greatest of all artist-craftsmen (*summus artifex*)," the soul is the Creator's workshop (*fabrica summi fabricatoris*). "Every good deed within it is like the most beautiful work" (LDO IV, 17). The edifice (*aedificium et templum*) is constructed from living bricks until it is completed (Sc III, 3).

A human being, according to Hildegard's contemporary Bernardus Silvestris, is so to speak the "workshop of nature," dedicated to "formation." Bernard of Clairvaux calls the universe a "great harp" that has to be continually tuned and readjusted with knowledge and wisdom. Wisdom is the "fragrant order" that resides in all works of art.

The Mother Abbess

Hildegard's description of a "capable," or virtuous, woman—the symbol of wisdom—in accordance with Proverbs (31:10) might well be a self-portrait. May all children of God (she implies) who find out how problematical life really is be fortunate enough to come across a woman of this kind: one who discards everything weak and ineffectual and acts prudently and resolutely. "She never tires and no road is too long for her take in search of the right answer to a question. Her inner resources never fail. A really capable woman knows how to distinguish between heavenly and earthly concerns (*spiritualia et saecularia*), and is wise and judicious in all her dealings (*sapienter agit omnia quae facit*). She takes all necessary measures, follows them through until they are carried out precisely, and protects those entrusted to her care, making sure that they do not appear naked before their Maker. Accordingly she is constantly active and loyal and as trustworthy as a ship must be to carry and distribute the goods and nourishment of life to other people. In this way all those in search of health and wholeness are encouraged, revitalized, and achieve the full satisfaction that ensures they will never again hunger or thirst" (LVM IV, 36-38).

Exercising such wisdom and foresight, for several decades Hildegard carried out the far from negligible duties of administering a community of nuns and caring for those entrusted to her, as when she comforted and reassured a discouraged nun: "Anyone who ploughs the field of her body with due discretion will not suffer when the end suddenly arrives but be received into the music of the Holy Spirit and enter a life lived in joy (*vita laeta*)" (PL 214 C). Guibert of Gembloux wrote about the admirable attitude to life in Hildegard's exemplary convent. He described the unusual perfection of the place in terms of "all the virtues (*ordo virtutum*) clearly vying for supremacy," and recalled his inability to decide whether the mother or the daughters outdid one another in excellence.

Hildegard grew particularly fond of one of these daughters to whom she was "mother in the spirit," and referred to her specifically as "my daughter." "She was a person," Hildegard wrote, "who filled my whole soul with love for her." She was like a flower "rich with beauty, fragrance and harmony." Hildegard felt united with her in "loving friendship" and admitted: "I do not know why you have deserted me like an orphan. I loved your noble conduct, your intelligence, your chastity, your soul, and the whole of your life—so much so that many people said to me: What are you doing?" But Hildegard felt compelled by the "living light of God" to treat her colleague and friend with the same spirit of love that dictated the tenor of her writings.

After her sudden separation from this friend, Richardis of Stade (a noblewoman and gifted collaborator with Hildegard in the transmission of her visions, who was appointed abbess of a Benedictine convent in the north of Germany), her mother in God poured out her pain in a letter: "I am overcome with anguish. My pain is so great that it quite destroys the great trust and wipes out all the comfort that I found in another human being." "But," as she recognized: "we ought to look to the living Lord on high for light wholly unshaded by any love or inadequate consolation of the kind offered by the dark air of this earth. When you think of God like that you look up to him like an eagle to the sun, which is very different from respect and affection for a noble person of this world, whose comfort, in the way of things, must fail just as flowers wither and fall. I did not rely on that perfect trust in God because of my love for just such a noble individual. And, I assure you, whenever I have gone wrong in this way God has let me suffer distress or grief that showed me where I had failed. And this is exactly what has happened because of you, as you are well aware" (Bw 98). At the same time Hildegard recognized the need to work through her grief: to accept the "gift of tears" (*donum lacrimarum*). Eventually she was able to write to Richardis: "I have banished this bitter mortal pain from my heart" (Bw 100).

Hildegard's motherly concern for her nuns was recognized far beyond the bounds of the Rupertsberg convent, for she extended it to all sorts and conditions of people. On one occasion, however, when Archbishop Hillin of Trier asked his "beloved sister" and "wise mother" Hildegard "in the fullness of your motherly heart, and for the sake of holy love, to allow a few drops from the wine-cellars of the Lord whose joyful plenty has already so enriched you in this life, to reach this sinner for his comfort" (Bw 49), we can detect a certain degree of satisfaction—or at least of gentle irony—in Hildegard's reply: "Yes, how true, for though a man certainly has more creative power than a woman, a woman is a source of wisdom and a fountain of joy, and both of these are necessary to make a man fully human!" "Unfortunately," she resolutely concluded, "because of that the present age is neither cold nor hot but just tepid." But things would become even more dire if as a result of irrepressible "male waywardness" wrong followed wrong on each of the four winds! (Bw 50).

Nevertheless, even if the state of things were to take such a disastrous turn—as seemed only too possible—she would remain steadfast and say and do what seemed obviously right: "I shall not yield to this earthly fragility (*fragili terrae*) but manfully strive to overcome my weak nature. If the works of injustice threaten to rise up in me, I shall summon the wisdom born of patience (*sapientia patientiae*) and conquer blood, flesh, and bone. Whatever happens I shall fight as bravely as a lion when its very life is at stake" (Sc I, 4).

23. Hildegard
Painting from a charter
of 13 July 1342

Joy and hope are fundamental qualities. They illumine the whole universe, and accompany us to our benefit in all the stages of our life, however endangered it may be. They are always there potentially, however wretched the circumstances. The hope that so to speak resounds in each human being leads straight to joy, which is the basic tenor of nature and the authentic attitude of any human creature. Hildegard never loses her sensitivity to nature. She is constantly overjoyed by its inexhaustible richness; by the fullness and fruitfulness of all existence; and by all the beauty that life offers us so that we can rejoice in, with, and at it. For her the whole world is essentially fresh, vital, and beautiful to behold; it is always lively with delight and expectation, for the beauty of greenness (*pulchritudo viriditatis*) runs through all that is (LDO IV, 12).

Divine harmony resounds in all forms of creation, but the most wonderful of all its manifestations is the human body, the place where we can most obviously recognize the divine principle itself. Life is filled with a divine music that makes it sing with beauty. Life is a profound and lasting melody, a radiant, sweet-tasting mystery that is all glorious within. The world as Hildegard sees it is replete with unmistakable images and instances of light, love and joy.

Wisdom and beauty, light and love are the sources of Hildegard's language and its ability to affect us. Her poetic sensibility reinforces her keen intellect and far-ranging imagination to the point at which the joy she felt pierces through the centuries in between. We best appreciate Hildegard when we look at nature, human and extra-human, in her spirit, and see that all things are potentially joyous, as they were meant to be.

In Praise of Joy

Hildegard certainly had to suffer pain and sorrow, harsh trials, and bitter disappointments, yet her life was essentially a single and unique hymn in praise of joy.

She saw joy as reigning over the world when it came into being. "For all magnificence, all joy and every sound uttered by the voice of life rejoicing in its intended fullness come from God alone" (LVM VI, 65). God is joy itself. But God did not want to keep his beauty and majesty for himself alone: "He wanted to give the light of his glory to his creatures, so that they could rejoice with him" (LVM I, 136).

Accordingly, human beings can never achieve perfect joy and happiness by their own efforts or from their own resources; they have to accept them as a gift from someone else: "When a person acknowledges and responds to the happiness offered by another human being, then his or her heart all but bursts with joy (*exsultatio magna*). For this acknowledgement and response is the soul remembering that God created it" (LDO VI, 51). "Then true joy wells up in a person's heart, because he or she knows that the other person has found happiness in mutual recognition and giving."

The Son of man felt this joy, "like a bridegroom who rejoices when he welcomes his bride into the love-nest of his heart" (LVM IV, 32). "What overwhelming joy that caused God to become a human being!" He resides as God among the angels yet is present among us in human form and in the ways proper to human beings (LDO V, 43).

All the works of God shine out from his heart and never grow old as the ages pass: "God was so rapturously happy in himself that he spoke his Word and called the whole creation into being. Then he rejoiced at what he had made, and was rapturously happy in what he had made!" The heart of true love is the very core and essence of the whole world, and in one of Hildegard's miniature dramatic dialogues maintains its authenticity as against "love of the world" in the wrong sense: "I am a pillar of heavenly harmony in which all vital joy is cconcentrated. I do not scorn true life" (LVM I, 11).

Hildegard never expressed the least disdain for a life lived in real joy and happiness. For her each new day was a ready source of things to be seen or heard that were or could become occasions of authentic delight. Again and again, as we make our way through her works, we see how the Sybil of the Rhine, "though suffering from painful illnesses from the instant of her birth," constantly experienced moments of joy (*vita laeta*). The virtue of "contentedness" enables her to affirm: "I am raised to sit as it were above the stars, because I am contented with all God's gifts. I delight in the sweet music of trumpets because I trust in God. I kiss the sun in joy because I know Him. I embrace the moon because my heart loves him. Everything that grows on the earth is sufficient for my needs. Therefore I dwell in the King's royal palace, and I lack nothing that my heart desires" (LVM V, 13).

For Hildegard, joy is the meaning of all experience. It is the divine gift of the beauty and savour of life that deserves incessant praise. Melancholy, however, destroys the "soul's buoyancy" (Sc I, 4). She says of the month of November that "its sad days pass coldly far from summer's joys" (LDO IV, 98). The blessed rejoice in the music of God's harmony "as someone might delight who sees the sun's splendour with his or her own eyes for the first time" (LVM VI, 44).

We should look up at the sun, moon, and stars and consider "how fortunate and happy we are to possess all these things that God has given us" (LVM V, 16). In fact "we already enjoy our heavenly home, but here on earth, if we are sensitive to the flowering of lilies and roses and to all the world's green freshness." There is joy to be found even in the midst of sadness, "and wherever there is joy we can find happiness" (LVM V, 17). "O blessed happiness!" she sings in her "In Loving Praise of Heavenly Things": "O sweet life! O tender embrace (*dulcis amplexio*) of everlasting life! There you can linger for ever in true delight. I can never stop rejoicing in this inner happiness!" (Sc III, 3).

"In this way the souls of the just are raised up to joy and advance to life through life" (LVM II, 43). The beneficial action of the soul shines out like the sun, which is at its height at midday. "Whenever our body does just and good works the soul rejoices at the thought of eternal life" (LDO IV, 30), and longs for life's true happiness, the "pleasures of our salvation."

In all sad occasions of this life, however miserable, we can still sense, if we will, "the atmosphere of light and joy." Everything physical is a source of joy under the governance of the human spirit, and joy turns life despite all unhappiness into a well-tuned "harp of the mind." Hildegard values a "full life that never decays in its youthful beauty and is not exhausted in the maturity of age" (LVM I, 11).

As we might expect, Hildegard celebrates the "splendour of heavenly joys" throughout her major visionary works. "At the end of the ages, freed from the burden of a fragile body, the just will be raised up to enjoy the height and breadth of radiant happiness joyfully and cheerfully" (LVM III, 40). "For after the resurrection of the body they will be granted even greater joys than they receive now on earth. At present they can only enjoy one aspect of their existence, but then, with both body and soul together, they will taste unutterable pleasures that no mortal creature can depict" (LVM VI, 58).

"And God will grant them all joy and happiness" (LVM VI, 7), those "joys in full measure" that the angels already knew but human tongues cannot describe (LVM VI, 25). Then, finally, the "joy of all joys" will resound in the "splendour of a happiness that knows no bounds but its own, for it is all in all" (LVM VI, 29).

Holy breath of holiness and fire-brand of love!
Heart's joy flowing in sweet and fragrant virtue!
Clear glass in which we see God claim the lost
And bring home all those who are forgotten!
Saving way that knows no rock or barrier,
You are in the highest, lowest, deepest.
You join all that is, all who are.
Through you clouds billow and winds blow,
The earth bears fruit and springs burst forth.
Through you the world grows green with promise.
You lead us through the wastes of this world
And guide us through this life's darkness.
You breathe your wisdom into us,
Filling us with joy and gladness.

(S 137)

24. Hildegard and her Assistants

The fiery stream of divine inspiration pours down as if through a tiny window and fills the upturned countenance of Hildegard waiting to record her visions. Behind her is the self-effacing figure of her beloved and devoted Sister Richardis. Separated from her cell, the monk Volmar is making a fine copy on parchment of what Hildegard has already inscribed on a wax tablet.
Liber Divinorum
Operum, *c.* 1240
Ms 1942,
Lucca, Biblioteca Statale

Education and training

Like Cassiodorus in Italy, Rabanus Maurus in Germany, and Isidore of Seville in Spain, Hildegard of Bingen lived and worked in the spirit of the Rule of St Benedict. She was profoundly influenced by monastic spirituality. Naturally she was well acquainted with the *lectio divina*, the daily reading of the scriptures, which are the only works directly quoted in her own writings. A great deal of Hildegard's language is either modelled on that of the Bible or is reminiscent of medieval biblical exegesis. In addition there are many passages that suggest knowledge of specific works by the Fathers of the Church and others that echo the ideas of contemporary philosophers and theologians. Nevertheless, there is no direct indication of exactly which sources Hildegard may have drawn on in the rich tradition of texts used in medieval education. Many of her influences may have come to her indirectly. On the whole, on the conceptual level at least, it is difficult to make precise distinctions between much of the foregoing and what Hildegard experienced herself, grasped intuitively, and reworked in her visionary style.

Nevertheless, a close analysis of her vocabulary supports the impression that she was thoroughly versed in the ideas of the Fathers and in those of several contemporaries. One might say that there is a subtext to much of her writing that is best summarized as a muted dialogue between Ambrose, Augustine and Lactantius, Rabanus, Isidore and Cassiodorus, the Venerable Bede and Scotus Erigena, Honorius of Regensberg and Hugh of St Victor, Wlliam of St Thierry and Rupert of Deutz, perhaps the rather dry works of Ivo of Chartres or even Gratian, and of course Gregory the Great and, inevitably, St Benedict.

Hildegard not only knew the text of the Rule of St Benedict but followed its practical directives throughout most of her life. She meditated on the liturgy and read and re-read the Bible every day. She knew the main ideas of the great Fathers of the Church as received and interpreted in her period, and she conducted a correspondence with some of the major scholars of her time. She was also fortunate in having highly-cultivated colleagues at close hand: the monk Volmar for some decades; the nun Richardis of Stade; and also, especially in the closing years of her life, the learned monk Guibert—from Gembloux, a monastery in Flanders.

As for her vast knowledge of natural science and lore, in this respect she was certainly greatly indebted to Bishop Siward of Uppsala. For some time, around 1135, the bishop was at the Disibodenberg monastery, for he consecrated three altars there. After his death (in 1156) he left behind an impressive library including a treatise on herbs (*Herbarium*), a book on precious stones (*Lapidarium*), several medical manuscripts, and the *Etymologiae* of Isidore of Seville, who became archbishop of Seville in about 600, and was known to his contemporaries as "the wisest man of modern times." This "Book of Etymologies" was the *Encyclopedia Britannica* of the entire Middle Ages, an attempt at a compendium of all human knowledge.

Of course Hildegard would also have drawn on the conventional literary resources of her period. Her style obeys the notions of correctness obtaining at that time, and she uses existing well-proven structures of presentation in order to put her statements in an appropriate sequence, to contrast and compare viewpoints, and so on. The very originality of her style and approach relies on these basic conventions and stands out all the more because there is an underlying structure of this kind. The wonder and mystery of her insights, visions, and predictions, her sudden surprising admonitions or recommendations, the way in which she combines useful instruction with totally captivating prose-poetry, all these and other unique aspects of Hildegard's works are often effective because of their rather ordinary setting. This is often the case with great works of art.

One of the most original devices of Hildegard's style is her use of sensuous imagery to appeal to all our senses: sight and hearing, smell and taste, and touch all the way from glancing sensuous impressions to holding and grasping, so that we seize things in their totality. Our apprehension is guided and manipulated so that it becomes rather like a bird in flight or a hermeneutical spiral of acquaintance and inquiry. It starts from the ground and rises to the highest point to survey the whole prospect, then falls gently, proceeding from the part to the whole, then from the whole to the parts, now pausing to consider the effects, then moving back again to the causes. In this constantly twisting, winding, but also extending and widening, spiral of images we continually meet with the same basic phenomena, but always on a different level. The whole process is, or rather creates, something like a highly complex and versatile spiritual and intellectual computer program, but one that demands the involvement not only of, say, our visual faculty but of our heart, if there is to be any useful outcome.

The visionary author herself is deeply involved in her perception of the beauty of God. She is affected by it "just as the string of a lute or harp is expertly touched by the player, so that the sound does not emerge from the string itself but from the player's action on it." That is how Hildegard perceives God's beauty in everything in this world, and sees the Creator everywhere in his creation. "How beautiful your eyes are," she says in *Scivias*, "when you proclaim what God has done, and when they are illumined by the dawn of what God has decreed." This perception of beauty is a response to the "fundamental resonance of the very depths of the cosmos," the "source in the Father's heart of unfailing light." It is the "primal image" shaped by God's own life-giving energy, the vital freshness of his love. It is *viriditas digiti Dei*—the "greenness of God's finger."

It is important to recall these mystical experiences when considering Hildegard's own illness. She realized that here on earth people have no kind of security about their individual future or about the past. We are mystified, blind, and deprived of certainty (*nullam securitatem*). All our actions seem ambiguous and doubtful (*omnia opera incerta*). All the days of humanity pass without precise assurance and disappear into oblivion. Only eternal life is stable, ever-new (*stabilis et nova*), and ever-fruitful.

When she talks of misery and suffering Hildegard uses terms proper to a range of reactions between perplexity and injury. She very often represents humans as *homo mutabilis*: helplessly subject to change in the particular medieval sense of "mutability;" victims of a mixture of restlessness and insecurity (*vitia instabilitatis*), and of aimlessness (*evagatio mentis*) at the crossroads of earthly cares (*in quadrivio curarum saecularium*); and burdened with all the miseries of this "shipwrecked" world.

This is the existentially unstable background to Hildegard's own ills. We constantly learn from her letters, from the Life by her biographers, and from her own accounts in different works that she was subject to severe illness. The infirmity and fragility of her body, according to Archbishop Philip of Cologne, disturbed and alarmed her heart, and Hildegard was never able to free herself completely from this "fearsome insecurity." God himself had ordained that she should not be safeguarded from this life's uncertainties "even in the midst of all its joys" (V II,5).

"I have never managed to lie down and enjoy a peaceful rest. Instead I have had to contend with a whole range of afflictions. The pains I suffered from the dry heat kneaded my body as if it had been no more than clay and water" (V II, 14). "On one occasion," she says, "I was so affected in this way that the blood in my veins dried up, the marrow in my bones shrivelled, and my bowels were rent, so that my whole body withered as when grass loses its fresh greenness in winter" (V III, 23). To Hildegard in this apparent sickness unto death it seemed that evil spirits were laughing and jeering at her condition: "Just look at her! She'll soon be gone and her friends lamenting will be all that's left of her!" Even though she was so utterly downcast, the prophetess learned, her soul would not be released, and further suffering awaited her.

"I am very prone to sickness and often so

afflicted by severe pain, that I feel I am about to die" (Bw 227). "My soul was so seriously affected that I almost died prematurely" (Bw 114). "I was cast down by illness and so exhausted that I could hardly stand on my feet, wretched woman that I am" (Bw 173). Even in her famous letter to St Bernard she acknowledged that she was "miserable as I am, and more than miserable, for I am just a woman." From childhood she had never known a moment's peace: "Never, not even for an hour" (Bw 25).

In addition to such general descriptions Hildegard offers quite detailed accounts of particular critical situations that many commentators have interpreted (and more often misinterpreted) in psychological and psycho-analytical terms. For instance, Hildegard reports: "My eyes were obscured for so long that I could no longer stand the light. The pressure on my body seemed so great that I could not get up. I lay there in terrible pain. But I had to suffer this condition because I refused to reveal the vision that I had been allowed to see" (V II, 5).

Hildegard suffered one severe attack of this kind for three years. "My whole body felt as if it had been baked in an oven" (V II, 26). People commiserated with her and helped her. She thanked God for making sure they were not absolutely sick of her. "But if the fierce physical pains I suffered had not been sent by God I could not have gone on living" (V II, 10). Whenever "out of fear of people's reactions I did not follow the way God had pointed out, this physical anguish increased"; the pain faded only when she obeyed. This finding is typical of Hildegard's accounts of her suffering: "But when I started writing I recovered my strength and rose up from my sick-bed."

At this juncture she mentions her creative reaction to being ill and to suffering and her confidence about recovery: "Like a mother who has just given birth, I can now talk again after my illness" (PL 128 B: *et sicut pariens post laborem, ita loquebar post dolorem*). "And just as earlier I had cried with pain, now I shed tears of joy, because God had not forgotten me" (V II, 5).

Once again Hildegard tries to define this tendency to suffering when she acknowledges that she is "a poor creature lacking all health and force, strength and education, just a

shadow of energy," a veritable sufferer (*homo patiens*), who is nevertheless fortunate enough to encounter *Christus Medicus*, the Great Physician (*magnus medicus*) "who encourages those who are awake, shakes those who are dozing, and lets those who persist in evil slip into the void" (PL 350 B).

"And so, gently, sensitively, respectfully and modestly (*leniter, suaviter, verecunda et humiliter*), Hildegard proclaimed the message of divine mercy manifested in her without any action on her part. For she considered it only proper to avoid praising her own capacities" (V III, 2), as her biographer puts it. Her young colleague Guibert constantly marvelled at the fact that: "Her achievements were exceptional, in spite of the burden of age and all her ill health, so that she could repeat with the apostle: 'Most gladly therefore will I rather glory in my infirmities, that the power of Christ may rest upon me'."

Her basic attitude to suffering is an essential key to the nature of her vision. "For she herself" (as she writes in the epilogue to her great cosmic prose-poem) "lives quite without security, and even with no scholarly under-standing of the scriptures, those strong walls for a mighty city which the Holy Spirit has provided to instruct the Church. From the day of her birth this woman has been bound by grievous sickness as if in a net, suffering constant pains in her veins, bones, and flesh. Yet to this moment God has not seen fit to release her from suffering, for she perceives some of his mysteries spiritually, peering through the aperture of her rational soul.

"This visionary power (*visio*) runs so fiercely through her veins that she is often greatly exhausted. At times it affects her slightly; at others it grows more severe and she is very ill. Consequently, she does not live like others but pursues a life of service under the inspiration of the Spirit. Her physical constitution comes from the air, and her sickness is so to speak imprinted in her by the atmosphere, the rain, the wind, and every change in the weather. She cannot rely on her own physical resources. Yet that is the only way in which she can receive the inspiration of the Spirit.

"Occasionally, however, by the great power of his goodness the Holy Spirit restores her from mortal sickness as if with life-giving dew, so that she may continue to serve the incoming of that same Spirit in human time. Yet

Almighty God truly knows every detail of this woman's suffering. May he so perfect his grace in her, in all his loving-kindness and to the greater glory of his goodness, that on leaving this world for ever her soul may be accepted and crowned by his mercy, and thus rejoice in everlasting glory. But the Book of Life, the writing of the Word through which all creation came into being, and of the Word that breathed forth all life as the eternal Father willed and ordained, miraculously produced what is written here; not through any teaching of human knowledge, not through any scholar, but through a simple woman.... May God be praised in all his works" (LDO X, 38).

The nature of vision

"Write what you see and say what you hear!" was the message of the mysterious voice that Hildegard obeyed in the decisive phases of her life. She was to write down exactly what she saw and heard: which meant words like leaping flames and images like clouds in the heavens.

Hildegard experienced her first powerful vision when she was forty-three years of age: "Trembling and utterly fearful, my spirit braced itself to receive what I saw." She attuned her sensibility to the nature of her vision and began to respond like a "tuba" or trumpet being played by some other being. Her biographer tells us (V II, 2) that

all this happened just as in the Song of Songs (5, 4): "My beloved put his hand to the latch, and my heart was thrilled within me."

A fiery light descended like lightning from the open sky. "It poured through my brain and like a flame through my heart and breast." Suddenly she realized the first implications of what was happening to her. She had to be alert: she had to experience everything with total receptivity and attentiveness, yes, but in full consciousness and making every attempt to understand, "with the eyes and ears of the inner person." Initially she rejected what was demanded of her and had to take to

her sick-bed, until at last, "compelled by so much suffering," she began to write. Then she recovered, but she could complete the work only with great effort. She had to spend ten long years composing her first great visionary work, which she called "Know the Ways of the Lord (*Sci vias Domini*)."

Hildegard was sixty and had reached the high-point of her work as an abbess when the voice from heaven told her: "From childhood you have been instructed in true visionary insight through the Lord's Spirit, not physically but spiritually. From this point, you are to proclaim what you now see and hear. From the start of your visions some things became apparent for you like fluid milk; whereas others were shown like a light, invigorating repast; and yet others like a full, solid meal. Now, yet again, you are to speak as I, not you, ordain; and you are to write as I, not you, say" (LVM 1).

This, as Hildegard herself records, happened "in the year 1158 after the Lord's birth, when the Holy See was severely oppressed and the emperor Frederick ruled over the Roman Empire." On this occasion too she was

profoundly moved by her vision: "My bodily senses were annulled and my perception was wholly transformed, as though I no longer knew who I really was! And my conscious mind received what seemed to be gentle drops of rain trickling from the imagination of God, just as the Holy Spirit bedewed the understanding of John the Evangelist."

Hildegard experienced this form of vision yet again, when she was sixty-seven. On that occasion too she was disturbed by her overpowering insights, and once more she became sick because of her tender and physically fragile constitution. "Yet again I heard the voice instructing me from heaven. It said: Write down what I say!" She obeyed her inward mentor: "This fragile, wretched creature began to write with a trembling hand, even though I was subject to various afflictions." Yet again she relied on her two collaborators, the monk Volmar and the nun Richardis, and "alert in body and senses" succeeded in writing out the mysteries disclosed to the inward eye of her spirit and to her inward ears.

Hildegard spent seven years on the composition of this last great visionary

25. John the Evangelist
Reims School, 1st quarter of the 9th century
Ebo Gospels, fol. 134v
Épernay, Municipal Library

enterprise. Once more the insights were accompanied by fear and trembling and by uncertainty about her own capacities, and they had to be converted to writing in spite of such obstacles as acute pain and mental crises. But she was also sustained by a simultaneous experience of immense pleasure and rejoicing. This eventually cancelled out all her anxiety and foreboding and left her with a lasting feeling of youthful joy.

God works as he wishes, to the honour of his name and not for the glory of mere mortals. And so I am always beset by fear and trembling, for I am not at all confident in my own abilities, but stretch out my hands to God so that he can hold me like a feather weighing nothing and subject to the wind's power.... I do not see these things with my outward vision or listen to them with my outward hearing. I see them only within, yet with my outer eyes open, so that I never become unconscious as in an ecstasy. I am fully awake when I see all this, by day and by night. The light I see is not confined by space. It is lighter and brighter than a cloud carrying the sun. This light has neither height, nor length, nor breadth. I am told that it is the "shadow of the living light."

What I see and learn in these visions I keep in my memory for a long time, so that when I see and hear this light I remember and simultaneously see, hear, and understand, as it were in that very instant, what I then know. But what I do not see I do not know or understand, because I am no scholar; I have only been taught to read the letters quite simply.... In this light I sometimes see another light that I am told is "the living light." When and how I see it I cannot say. But while I see it I am quite without sorrow and anxiety, so that I feel like a young girl and not like an old woman.

(Pi 332/333)

The German prophetess

At the height of her many-sided life and activity, Hildegard's most characteristic role would seem to have been that of prophetess or seer. Her contemporaries saw and admired her as *prophetissa teutonica*, as "the German prophetess" or Sybil. "Send me," wrote John of Salisbury, then still secretary to Archbishop Theobald of Canterbury, "the visions and prophecies of the blessed and celebrated Hildegard, who lives among you. She seems to me most worthy of renown and respect, especially since our Lord [Pope Eugenius III] has embraced her with particularly warm affection and confidence."

Though she was quite conscious of her visionary mission, Hildegard herself emphatically shunned any kind of banal soothsaying. She did not see her mission as revealing "future destinies" in order to satisfy mere human curiosity. Her only purpose was to transmit the "profundity of Holy Writ" that had been conveyed to her in her visions (Sc I, 3). Of course the transformation of the "ordinary trembling" of this "quite simple woman" into bold prophetic utterance did not occur instantly. It was preceded by a fundamental spiritual conflict or struggle, with counterparts in the experience of biblical prophets.

For others, too, in her lifetime she was a figure surrounded by a visionary aura, a general impression of what Hildegard herself called the "shadow of the living light," in which everything in the world was reflected as if in clear water and became a fitting image of reality. This reflection or "shadow" enclosed, or was a kind of stage for, the special visionary experiences, messages, and instructions which she felt compelled to obey and for which she was to become the unique vehicle. Hildegard was indeed a prophetess, in the sense of someone who submitted to an overpowering visionary force in fear and trembling. She did

so as if hypnotized by the light which she alone saw, and described herself as a captive "through whom the waters of God's mysteries flow" (LDO, introduction).

When we try to elicit the possible sources of Hildegard's knowledge and to distinguish them from her own creative additions we are constantly struck by what can only be called her prophetic stance, by the extraordinarily vibrant yet authoritative nature of her language, both in her narrative style and in the devices she uses to create and enhance its dramatic effects. This prophetic thrust seems to fade in the quasi-scholarly passages but always re-emerges as the dominant effect.

All ages and all cultures have thrown up forms of this visionary reflection of and on reality: from the *mantis* of the Greeks to the *kahin* of the Arab world. The original meaning of the Hebrew *propheta* is something like "one who is made to speak," and who is therefore the bearer of a message greater than the messenger. It is not wholly improper to compare Hildegard with the great prophets of the Old Testament and her pronouncements with their admonitions and proclamations—especially those of Jeremiah, whose sensitivity and modesty are very like the humble trembling of Hildegard when faced with her commission. She was similarly borne up by a conviction that she had been specially chosen and commanded to arouse people's consciences and that it was her duty to hand on God's own ideas and not some mere secular form of instruction.

Magistra Hildegardis most acutely defined the nature of prophecy in this sense and presented herself in the line of such great figures of the Old Covenant as Isaiah or Ezekiel when she wrote: "She appears with a certain hardness. It is like the rigidity of marble (*marmorea soliditas*). She flatters no one, for she is subject to the inflowing of the

26. *The Lord summons Jeremiah*
c. 1180
Winchester Bible,
fol. 148r
Winchester,
Cathedral Library

27. *The Vision of Isaiah*
Reichenau, late 10th
century
Commentary on the
Book of Isaiah,
Ms Bibl. 76, fol. 10v
Bamberg, Staatsbibliothek

A theology of music

In the Pythagorean-Platonic tradition of the West, music is a fundamental regulative principle for the education of individuals and for the due ordering of communal life. It was in this sense, as well as aesthetically, that it came to be thought of as a therapeutic medium. In accordance with this tradition—as accepted by Boethius and in particular by Isidore of Seville—Hildegard argues from the basic notion of a cosmic harmony that requires everything, macrocosm and microcosm, to be in tune. For her, the entire cosmos is a well-tuned musical composition. The idea is to be found in many aspects of Christian thought, especially in the notion of the history of salvation culminating in celestial harmony.

This concept lies behind Hildegard's hymning (entirely in line with the classical idea of *musica mundana*, or "earthly music") of all the elements of creation: "And fire proffers flames and is God's song of praise. And the voice is the word and it is praise of God.

Accordingly the whole creation is a single hymn in praise of God" (Pi 352). In this understanding the world and humanity are a perfectly concordant musical unity. In fact all Hildegard's words and songs are musical and stress the musicality of what they describe. For her the functions of nature and the passing of time are essentially harmonious; the music of nature is the music of time; and the whole cosmos is melodiously structured.

Furthermore, the invisible music of the heavenly bodies in motion, the music of the spheres (*musica mundana*), accords with the harmony of physical and psychological proportions in human beings (*musica humana*); and both are echoed in the rich symbolism of various instruments (*musica instrumentalis*). "Each element has its proper tone, its own timbre, the elementary sound of the order of God's creation. Yet all sounds unite in a single harmonious tonality as if issuing from so many harps and lyres." This beautifully-ordered primal melody also resounds in the

human soul. It is "the melody of that utterly beautiful sound which is the Sound of sounds" (LVM IV, 59). The sonorous symbolism of all being finds its due unity when orchestrated in the great overall "Symphonia," reflected in Hildegard's songs of praise with their antiphons, responses, and hymns.

"Therefore the whole celestial harmony rejoices in glorifying God and is enraptured to know that earthly humanity, though it comes from the earth, can look up to the heights where God dwells. All praise and all kinds of music resound above the heavens in praise of the marvellous things that God has brought about in humankind" (LDO V, 40). The full celestial symphony (*omnis caelestis symphonia*) has already issued from the Virgin's womb, and now creation as a whole rejoices (*in symphonia sonet*). All the harps of heaven (*caelestia organa*) resound, uniting in celestial harmony (*ad caelestem harmoniam*).

Music also rings out in angelic and saintly beings. The company

of angels lives in a state of praise (*laudando concinit*). They sing and rejoice in an eternal chorus of praise (*in laudibus sonant*). Everything shines forth in a resplendent melody (*in caelesti harmonia fulget*), and resounds in superlative harmony (*in superna symphonia*). And so the Holy Spirit sings and plays (*symphonizat Spiritus Sanctus*) in Rupert, Hildegard's favourite saint.

Hildegard herself provided the perfect saying to define this fundamental musical constitution when applied to human beings: "The human heart is harmonious (*anima symphonialis est*)." It originates in primordial and tends to ultimate harmony. We still possess the elementary tonality of divine order, sense all that is out of tune in our present state, and long for our eventual inclusion in the perfect symphony. But even now the company of heaven rejoices at every sound that every virtue makes. "Therefore we ought to rejoice in unison (*decet nos in symphonia sonare*)."

Before he lost the state of innocence, Adam's voice was in perfect tune with the voices of the angels singing God's praises. The angels formed a choral community, as their spiritual nature required. Adam lost this kinship through his guilt. But God wanted to restore the light that had been lost and to renew the primal harmony of creation. Longing for that same renewal, the prophets not only composed psalms and songs to arouse the devotion of those who heard them, but invented various musical instruments to accompany them tunefully. They did all this to exhort and train (*admoniti et exercitati*) the listeners and to edify them from within.

Therefore it is a grave matter to forbid the singing of God's praises (*canticum laudum*). For, just as the Holy Spirit summoned Jesus' body into being in Mary, so the praise of God in the Church, as an echo of celestial harmonies, has its roots in the Holy Spirit. Therefore God is to be praised with sounding cymbals. On hearing a song, people so to speak breathe deeply and sigh; this constantly reminds us that the soul too has its origin in heavenly harmony.

(PL 220 A-221 C: Letter to the Prelates of Mainz)

31. Allegorical Figures representing medieval Music:
Musica mundana
Musica humana
Musica instrumentalis
(from top to bottom)
c. 1300;
Florence, Biblioteca Laurenzia

32. Angelic Choirs
Liber Scivias, copy of the
former Rupertsberg
Codex,
c. 1180;
St Hildegard's Abbey,
Eibingen

65

33. **How the Creation came about**
The figure of Love, surmounted by fatherly Goodness, carries the Lamb, symbolizing tenderness. Love has exerted itself and produced the creation, which it now protects with its encircling wings while trampling evil underfoot.
Liber Divinorum Operum, *c.* 1240;
Ms. 1942,
Lucca, Biblioteca Statale

3. Light, life, and creation

A wholesome life

In Hildegard's visionary perception of the world love is always reported or shown as a particularly beautiful apparition or image. In an illustration to the "Book of Divine Works" she depicts it as a human being of unusually comely form, whose self-descriptive monologue she reproduces:

"I, the fiery life of divine essence, flame out over the beauty of the fields, shine in the waters, and burn in the sun, moon, and stars. With every breath of air I awaken all things to life. The air comes alive as nature grows green and blooms, and the waters flow as if they too were alive. The sun blazes as a living light, and the moon is kindled and constantly renewed by the sun's fire." For love is life. It is life whole and entire (*integra vita*): "not struck from stones, not blossoming from branches, and not rooted in a man's generative power." All life originates in love. "Its root is reason, so to speak, in which language sounds and flowers" (LDO I, 2).

Love, then, is not only a beauteous form but the elementary force which is expressed in all forms of life and is enunciated, takes effect, and becomes reality through the rational understanding. Divine life lies hidden in all reality. It is there as an underlying fiery force always striving to emerge; as an active fire that can be heard in words and has its origin in reason.

Hildegard always portrays the reality of this world in threefold form. Like the trinitarian Godhead, "Reason has three capacities: breath, sound, and word. The Son is in the Father as the Word in Sound. The Spirit is in both together as Breath and Word. And the Spirit of the Lord inspires the whole world in this way."

The voice of her personal revelation also tells her: "There are three powers in stone, three in flame, and three in the word. Moist greenness, palpable self-consistency, and the fire that ignites: all these reside in stone." Flame also has three powers in a single fire, just as the one God dwells in three Persons: "Flame burns in shining light, in purple breath, and in fiery glow." Similarly, there are three things at work in the word: sound, force, and breath: "Sounds enables the word to be pronounced; force allows it to be apprehended; and breath lets it reach its full power" (Sc II, 2).

Then Hildegard gives the comparison an unusually bold twist: "Similarly human beings possess three powers in their sexual capability: sexual desire (*concupiscentia*), sexual drive (*fortitudo*), and the sexual act (*studium*)." Libido enflames potency with ardour so that the sexual act is completed in mutual passion: "The expression of male desire depends on the will of God (*voluntas*), and the force of generation on God's power. Desire and potency become a single harmony when a man has sex with a woman, and male and female prolong the human race in unison and concord" (Sc III, 3).

Here Hildegard stresses the dependence of the creative power of the life-force on human decision and action. "Since God is rationality itself, how could he not be at work when he allows each and every one of his works to flower through humankind? For he created human beings in his own image and likeness, and designedly and duly inscribed each of his creatures in this humanity. For God had decided from eternity to create his work, which is humankind. And when he had completed this work, he handed the entire creation to human beings for them to work with thereafter, just as God himself had worked to make humanity. This is how human beings are the work of God (*opus Dei*)" (LDO I, 2).

Hildegard gives the almighty Creator God ruling over his creation a human form. Love is shown as a brilliant figure enclosing the whole world in the majestic span and scope of his wings, for the Creator communicates with his entire creation through his all-embracing love. Light streams out from his fiery-red face to enkindle all the beauties of the cosmos, for his love is irrepressibly full. As it overflows it expresses a light that penetrates and infuses all creation with wholesome life.

The fire of God's love runs through the world and its beauties, constantly re-enlivening the cosmos as a miracle of perfection (*elegantissima ordinatio*) (LDO III, 46). Green roots, seedtime, flowering, and beauty are essential aspects of nature's radiant substance. "Every creature possesses some part of this divine illumination, which is exhibited in its greenness, budding, and blossoming, and in the beauty of its being! Otherwise it could not exist as part of creation" (LDO IV, 11). Greenness (*viriditas*) produces flowers, and flowers yield fruit. Clouds move on their way. The moon and the stars scintillate with the power of this radiant light. Wood may seem to grow dry and wither yet then grows fresh and green as new shoots spring forth. Water wells up and sparkles airily then pours out in streams (PL 171 A). The revivification of creation by the life-force is a never-ending process.

Human beings occupy an exemplary position and play the part of mediators in the midst of this creation produced in and from the living light. They exist in creation, in the midst of all living things, just as God's Son dwells in the Father's heart (*in medio corde Patris*) (LDO IX, 9). The intimate alliance between the world and humankind is the sole guarantee of the order of the cosmos. This association is apparent in each person, where it takes the form of a special reflection of the world as a whole (*omnis creatura*) (LDO II, 32). This luminous reality also appears as a vital principle in every aspect of the human organism (LDO IV, 105), filling people with life and radiating an atmosphere of vitality roundabout them (LDO IV, 105).

God, of course, is not a slumbering fire or hidden glow but a constant source of energy. "He creates rational life so that the eyes see, the ears hear, the nose smells, and the mouth utters real words of reason" (LVM I, 37). God did not wish to keep his glory to and for himself. "He wanted to communicate himself to his creatures so that they could rejoice with him. He did this just as a hen takes her chicks under her wings" (LVM I, 36).

God proclaims and summons. He is an urgent, living voice, an ardent fire and the source of all truly rational thought and behaviour. The God of revelation is a living God. He wishes to be heard by reasonable people and asks for openness and for an appropriate response. Human beings are images of God only if they respond duly to God conceived in this way. The Father speaks, the Son answers, and the Holy Spirit is the loving orientation of this eternal conversation between Father and Son.

This enlightened understanding of reality is a special privilege of human beings. They alone are aware of it in this particular way. God has given them a rational mind (*rationabilis vita*) and has thereby placed them in the company of angels. This basic ability enables humans to perceive and discriminate in all respects (*rationalitas discernit omnia*). They examine, study, investigate and interrogate everything (*subtiliter penetrat et discutit*). Only by acting thus does the rational human being become a being able to decide for himself or herself, and to bear due responsibility for his or her decisions and actions.

Human reason is like a sonorous trumpet that gives people the "power to exult." The human soul is also a "well-tuned, effectively resounding (*symphonizans*) master-instrument" (LVM IV, 59). The exercise of reason keeps people rationally alive.

God loved these rational beings so much that he decided to give them the position and privileges once enjoyed by the fallen angels whom he had had to banish: "He accorded them all the glory and honour that the angels lost when they surrendered their blessed state" (LDO I, 3). God decided to endow this specially designated creation, humanity, with a particular form—to enclose humans in his loving embrace, as it were, so that they received a special divine shape as he formed them from the dust of the earth: "I have embraced this work of mine with great love and special affection. Through the fire of my Spirit I have transformed humankind, given them bodies, and presented them with the whole world to command" (LVM VI, 52).

Of course "no human being can possibly know in his or her lifetime" the truly profound nature of so mysterious a course, so beautiful an existence, so joyful a life. The mysteries of revelation and all that we are told are merely shown to us "as if through a window (*quasi fenestraliter*)," or as if reflected in a glass darkly (*quasi per speculum*)" (LVM VI, 65).

Many of the images that Hildegard offers us in her visionary pictures and words are indeed views through windows and reflections in mirrors, but—to change the metaphor somewhat—they are also explorations of the texture of the great cosmic veil woven from love that envelops all that is.

Love is also the keynote of the great passionate hymn that proclaims the inner relationship between the Creator and his creation. With loving lips God kisses his own work (*officiale opus*) and embraces it intimately (*amando amplexus*). The Creator addressing his creation is like a lover talking to his beloved. God's love is a gift intended for and offered to humanity.

Hildegard represents herself as full to overflowing with her vision of this beautiful world produced by God's love and suffused with the living light. She constantly acknowledges the personal joy and happiness she has experienced in her particular act of mediation: "How fortunate, how happy I am! The Lord Jesus Christ prepares me and makes me a creature of light; he adorns me and makes me beautiful because I so long for the Lover whom I wish to embrace for ever and to possess in joy, in and beyond all things" (Sc III, 6).

The life of the one God in three Persons

In the brightness of the living light Hildegard perceives a sparkling sapphire-blue human form that also emits a gently glowing red fire. The figure is bathed in light and fire. All three, light, fire and form, are made manifest in a single radiance of unequalled power.

But these Instances or Persons are *one* God in a single undivided Godhead. God showed his love to us in the form of his Son. "For through the Word, the very source of life, God's motherly love came down to embrace us" (Sc II, 2). Through the Word, his Son, the Father created all things in the Holy Spirit. And the Spirit, through whom all things grow fresh and green with the force of life (*viriditas*), dwells in the Father and in the Son. Together, "whole and immutable, forever undivided in unity, they compose a single Substance of inconceivable beauty" (Sc III, 7).

"Can two hearts possibly exist in one breast?" asks Hildegard, and she assures us: "Similarly, there cannot be two Gods in heaven" (Sc I, 2).

Hildegard's depictions of the "three Persons in One" are interchangeable and complementary. The Word, through whom in the Holy Spirit the Father created the universe, miraculously became flesh. In this way the God-Man raised human nature to the throne of God to dwell at the Father's right hand. The dust of the earth has returned to the bosom of God.

Severed from the original source of life, human beings reverted to their own nothingness. They were so to speak "sawn off from the joy of life" (Sc III, 7). But now the water of regeneration heals us spiritually and purifies our blood. For the blood too often tends to "run along the wrong paths in an agonizing sweetness that all too easily leads to burning lust." The salvific water that purifies us by removing everything filthy is a metaphor for the Son, who has redeemed us utterly by his suffering. "And the blood that circulates in humans and bestows its heat on them represents the Holy Spirit, who arouses and enkindles the noblest virtues in people" (Sc III, 7). In this symbolic image, too, the Spirit, the Water and the Blood "are three in one and one in three."

34. The God of Illumination

The Creator God enthroned at the summit of a mountain-range as Ruler of the universe. People with features appropriate to their attitudes peer in various directions from little window-apertures in different parts of the world. The figures of "Fear of the Lord" and "Poverty in the Spirit" appear against the background of the starry blue cosmos. The latter's face is obscured because irradiated by divine glory.

Liber Scivias, copy of the former Rupertsberg Codex, c. 1180; St Hildegard's Abbey, Eibingen

35. True Trinity in true Unity
A sapphire-blue prophetic figure surrounded by a brilliant light is suspended before a fiery golden disk. A silver stream emerges from a midnight-blue background to create unity out of trinity.

Liber Scivias, copy of the former Rupertsberg Codex, *c.* 1180; St Hildegard's Abbey, Eibingen

Hildegard also tells us how she was instructed to let others know about these mysteries and their implications: "Speak openly about the bread that is my Son. He is life in the midst of love's fire." But God does not merely give her information to adapt and hand on to people; some things he says are for her alone, though she repeats them too, in order to bring out the quality of his love: "How beautiful your eyes are when you talk of heavenly matters and divine wisdom is dawning in your mind!" (Sc III, 1).

Holy Wisdom in your power
Hold us fast in every hour.

Enclose us in your threefold wings
Spreading to embrace all things.

One pierces heaven's heights above,
Another touches earth with love.

The other moves with tender care
In mystery through the cosmic air.

Holy Wisdom in your power
Enlighten us in every hour.

(S 27)

36. The Head of God
A three-winged head looking fiercely northward represents the power of divine love.
Liber Scivias, copy of the former Rupertsberg Codex, *c.* 1180;
St Hildegard's Abbey, Eibingen

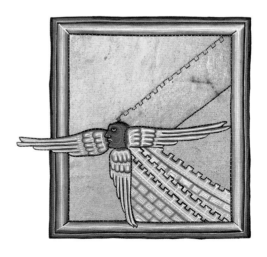

The universal wheel

Hildegard shows us the cosmos as a sphere suffused with love and radiating universal light. At its centre is the living human form. This she portrays as a powerful figure towering over and surpassing all other creatures, which by nature are wholly dependent on and obedient to the pre-ordained structure of creation. Moreover, human beings not only exceed all other creatures in stature but in a certain sense represent the whole creation (*omnis creatura*) in their physical being. They project over and beyond the earthly realm into another dimension where the universal elements of water, fire, and the winds hold sway.

Humanity is depicted as structurally one with the universal wheel or sphere. People are involved in a dense mechanism of hereditary characteristics and capacities, traits and tendencies, and in an equally real and fateful environment of conditions, states, and determining factors. They must conduct their lives as responsible individuals, orientate themselves and decide their destinies within the space of their freedom. But their frailty in this earthly life also requires them to use their gift of reason to obey the Creator's injunctions, and to take every opportunity offered them in order to achieve health, wholeness, and salvation.

"And so God has provided human beings with all the forces of nature. He has given them the instruments and functions of creation, so that with them they can interact with the world and with everything in it. They can perceive and recognize it by sight; listen to it and comprehend it by hearing; discern it and discriminate between its aspects by smell; consume it by taste; and control it by touch." This (as is the divine intention) should enable them to arrive at knowledge of the true God, who is the Lord of all worlds. God has shaped them in conformity with the structure of the world, just as an artist-potter fashions his vessels in accordance with a preconceived design. God has laid out the macrocosm, the gigantic instrument that is his universe, in compliance with judiciously-dimensioned plans. He has followed the same blueprints when assembling microcosmic humankind, whose layout conforms to that of the vast structure within which it operates: "God made human beings by fitting limb to limb, joint to joint, limb to joint, and joint to limb, so that each element in the variety of the whole moves in unison, whether at the neck, at the shoulders, at the elbows, at the hands, at the thighs, or at the knees and feet; and the same applies to the organization of every other part of their bodies" (LDO IV, 97).

This fundamental constitution means that each person must always be seen as a whole, in his or her entire physical being (*corpus ubique*), as God intended and as he contrived things from the beginning. Similarly, men and women are reciprocal beings and designed to relate to one another. In relation to each other they are address and response, operating in a complex system of mutual responsibility. In relation to all that is, human beings are the heart of creation, engaged in a perpetual dialogue with the world.

Humans use their reason, their intellect, the rational orientation of their sense-experience, and the organization of the concepts they derive from it in order to apprehend, to try, and to taste things and thereby to construct an appropriate picture of the world. Eventually, in this way, they arrive at a "world view" or philosophy of existence. They have to learn to see what is and what is what. Then they must appropriate whatever suits their purposes from what lies about them. Furthermore, they have to distinguish what is right from what is bad for them, so that they can make accurate, free, and responsible decisions. For this purpose

37. **Cosmic Humanity**
God the Father bears the great wheel of creation on his breast. It is supported and embraced by the figure of flaming Love. In the middle of the universal wheel stands a human being, projecting beyond the tiny earth into the realms of universal forces with their various elements and rays. The human figure seems to hold the universal network or system in its hands, thus accepting humanity's task of creative commitment to the world.
Liber Divinorum Operum, c. 1240; Ms. 1942, Lucca, Biblioteca Statale

humans have been given the gift of discernment, or discrimination (*discretio*), which gradually becomes true wisdom (*sapientia*). Their development and education result from due acquaintance and from judicious choice and give them the capacity to win refreshment and joy from everything in life. The world has immense variety and extraordinary beauty in store for mature human beings when they bring their properly nurtured gifts of rational apprehension and discrimination to bear on it.

"And God assigned the whole creation to humans so that they could investigate it, and understand (*penetrare*) it by means of their human faculties, and come to know and recognize all things. For a human being as such represents the whole creation (*homo omnis creatura*), and in him or her the breath of life, which is everlasting, is apparent in its fully-realized form" (CaCu 45, 17-20).

The human body and soul

God made human beings with the entire creation at their disposal, and He himself decided to assume "the clothing of human flesh and form." God's Word and the human body became a living unity in the same way that the body is the garment of the soul and the soul is designed to function together with the body. "The body would be nothing without the soul, and the soul could do nothing without the body. Consequently they form a unity (*unum*) in the human being and together constitute that which is human" (LDO IV, 105).

The soul is, as it were, the green freshness and life-force (*viriditas*) of the body (LDO IV, 21). Therefore the soul is happy and rejoices as it plays its part in the operations of life: "The body was shaped by God himself, and the soul is intent on carrying out the functions of the body (*opus corporis*)" (LDO IV, 19).

Nevertheless, no one knows precisely how the soul is so intimately bound up with the human body and blood that "they form a single life" (*una vita*) (Sc III, 7). We do know, however, that "the spirit cannot be a living human being without the physical matter of the blood, and that the substance of the blood in the body (*sanguinea materia corporis*) can never constitute a living human being without the soul's cooperation" (Sc III, 7).

Hildegard's view of the soul does not accord with that attributed to Augustine, who said:

"God and the soul, and nothing else!" (that is, human beings are "rational souls using mortal and earthly bodies"; the soul is a substance in itself, an immaterial principle which animates the body; and the soul's rational knowledge of God is intimately associated with its search for God as Truth). According to Hildegard, the soul (or mind) is neither situated at a particular point in the organism nor located anywhere outside the body. In her understanding it is certainly not imprisoned in the body, as Plato may be thought to have held; and it is not divorced from a number of physical processes in the human body, which to that extent would be a machine or automaton, as Descartes may be said to have argued. For Hildegard the soul does not aspire or try to free itself from this world. It does not seek to build even in this life some kind of heavenly retreat where it can take refuge and exist seemingly apart from this life. It realizes its nature and expresses its positive, constructive impulse in and through corporeal reality by striving to perfect the *opus corporis*, the work of the body.

Consequently, the soul is to the body as the sap is to a tree. "It extends through all the parts of a person, giving life to the marrow and veins and to all the limbs of the body, just as a tree draws sap from its root and thus infuses greenness into all its branches.... The soul's understanding is like the greenness of branches and leaves; the will is like blossoming; the heart is like ripening; and the reason like fully-mature fruit. In this way the soul strengthens and supports the human body" (Sc I, 4).

"Accordingly, in spite of their different natures, both body and soul exist as a single reality (*unum opus*). We see this unified reality (*opus*) at work when the soul supplies its physical organism with air in the process of thinking, with heat in the course of concentration, with fire in the assimilation of matter, with water in the material act of its incorporation, and with the life-force (*viriditas*) in the generative process. This is how human beings are composed. This is how they express their basic constitution and follow their original design (*a prima constitutione*). They exist as bodies (*corpus ubique*) above and below, within and without (*et supra et subtus, circa et intra*)—everywhere, in fact. For this is the fundamental nature of humankind (*et hoc est homo*)" (LDO IV, 103).

38. The Soul and its Pavilion (detail)
The child in its mother's womb receives its soul from God as if it were a ball of fire falling from heaven. Men and women present their gifts to the new life coming into being. Incarnation and Redemption—which the new human being will also share in—dawn in the golden quadrilateral sewn with eyes (a symbol of God's universal presence). Liber Scivias, copy of the former Rupertsberg Codex, *c.* 1180; St Hildegard's Abbey, Eibingen

77

The body is a universal medium that gives us physical access to the world. The implications should be clear from the following example. Our stomach—not so much the brain, and not even the heart—has the capacity to apprehend and process the world (*capax mundi*). In fact, we may see the entire universe as no more than a vast stomach which enables the substance of the world under various aspects to percolate through us (*capacitatem mundi ostendit*) in the course of our life. The stomach craves and assimilates the essential properties, or potencies, of the creatures which it receives in this way and then emits, thus maintaining a constant state of equilibrium and concordance with circumambient reality. Similarly, not only the stomach but all other parts of the body, from head to toe, are involved in a continuous reciprocal process of this kind. This is especially true of the sexual organs in all their ramifications. This process illustrates and expresses the great design announced in the prologue to the Gospel according to John. In fact it is an actual physical demonstration of the truth proclaimed there. It shows that the Word has become flesh; that it has done so limb by limb, organ by organ; and that this is exemplified in every man and woman, in every age of human history.

Humanity as male and female

Body and soul are inseparable, and so are man and woman. "God himself led man and woman to sexual union. He joined what was strong with the weak so that one would be held by the other". Things have been ordered thus, in a wholly upright way, from the beginning. There is no need for anyone to be ashamed of his or her sexual behaviour (Sc II, 6). Male and female are so intimately joined in this act that each one both fulfils the other and is actually remade by the other (*opus alterum per alterum*) (LDO IV, 100).

The sexual act is not the product of some kind of natural drive; it takes place as a creative act something like the practice of architecture: like the conception, design, and construction of a building (*aedificium*). The tempestuous passion of a man in sexual union with a woman makes him behave like a "ship on high seas; sexual desire seizes him like the burning of a volcano in full fire and tumult."

In a woman, however, sex is like "a small boat that, even if with some effort, can still be arrested in the midst of waves stirred up by soft breezes and in whirlpools aroused by light gusts of wind," or like "a wood fire you can easily put out." In contrast to the fury of male desire and love-making, female sexual advances and responses are like the "sound of a lyre" (CaCu 72. 34).

In this ultimately close relationship a man and a woman cling to one another, never want to part, are pulled together, indeed run to one another, are warmed by the heat of mutual desire, penetrate one another, and long and thirst for one another like the stag for fresh waters. They taste and explore one another's fullness and sweetness, unravel one another's nature and unburden themselves to one another, yet always retain a certain indecypherable mystery that draws them even closer together. They endure the disappointments, suffering, and pains of life together.

In their physical form human beings became storehouses of all God's wonders (*clausura mirabilium Dei*). Each human being is the work of God (*opus Dei*), and people were originally endowed with male strength in order to carry out their tasks. They became partners of the world (*opus cum creatura*), which henceforth provided their field of action and defined the horizon of their endeavours. But God gave the male human being a helpmate, a special partner to allow him to express his creative abilities: a being who would respond to him, dwell with him, and whom he too would dwell with and accompany through life. She would be a physically loving spouse and enable them to rejoice in one another and fulfil one another, so that the man and the woman could be truly one another's work and re-creation (*opus alterum per alterum*). Man and woman "are one flesh in loving union." Therefore "they should remain righteously united (*in rectitudine coniunctionis*), and not rend each other like vipers but cleave to one another in the embrace of love" (Sc I, 2).

People are intended to live on the earth and make their home there as physical and sexual beings and to enjoy the pleasures of life (*vita laeta*) together with all other creatures. That was the purpose of God's "initial planting" of the earth (*plantatio prima*), the world's wedding, as it were. For God gave the woman to

*39. **Conrad of Alstetten***
A pair of lovers against a
background of deep-red
roses symbolizing courtship

Codex Manesse,
Cod. Pal. Germ. 848,
fol. 249 v (detail);
Heidelberg, University
Library

79

the man, so that there should be knowledge and joy. "Full joy in life should prevail between man and woman: that perfect love that already flowered in the first human couple" (Sc I, 2). By making love (*opus*) together, they would fulfil one another, give one another a means (*verbum*) of self-expression, and share in the mystic life-force (*viriditas*). *Opus verbi viriditas*, the fresh and vital articulation of the Word, amounts to Hildegard's definition of married life in threefold mystery, for a human being is simultaneously the bride of nature, his or her own partner, and a sharer in creation.

Henceforth, together with the rest of creation, humanity will enjoy life through every sense: "The eyes are windows of the soul and channels of experience. The ears are wings of perception and understanding and instruments of reason. The nose is a tool of discrimination and the mouth conveys the taste of reality, allowing things to be licked and giving humans the power to sense their inner essence, just as the hands allow them to act fully and meaningfully." Eating and drinking are the means by which the elements are exchanged. Breathing never stops and keeps people in continuous union with the cosmos. As the central organ of metabolism, the stomach detects and indicates the capacity of the world. And people are granted sleep for inward rumination, for communion with the inner self. "And so God established human beings in community and partnership with all existence." People are the bearers of being (*omnia fert*) and shepherds of existence, yet all creatures and all aspects of creation exist together with humans and, indeed, *in* the very acts and ways in humans are human beings (*omnis creatura in eo est*).

On the basis of this natural constitution (*opus Dei*) and through all their interhuman relations (*opus alterum per alterum*) human beings perceive and understand their own special task in the external world (*opus cum creatura*). No person relies on himself or herself alone or exists for self alone. He or she is dependent on something above, responsible for him, for her, for them, and oriented to the outside world. People find their purpose and duty in the world and conduct a meaningful dialogue with it, not only by means of their biological intentionality and equipment, their "programming," but by virtue of their purposeful impulse to be unique individuals, their personal directedness.

People also live creatively. They themselves are created, but they also create themselves, that is, become fruitful, through what they make and do (*operans factum opus in operatione*). All their virtues are the work of those who live and work in God (*opus operantis hominis in Deo*) (Sc III, 3). From the beginning God allowed his creatures to shine forth creatively in this way. "And he not only led them to the light, but allowed them to develop evermore toward the point of true perfection (*ad perfectionem*)" (LVM I, 47).

Divine life gives everyone and everything in creation the fruitfulness needed to evolve, for everything is intended to mature and ripen to full perfection (*ad completionem perfectionis*). Everything has to become: to unfold in the process of coming to be. It has to develop creatively from the essence of its own being (LVM III, 28), which means to proceed outward. For everything ordained by God is reciprocal: it speaks and responds to everything else in living mutuality, and thus declares its own particular responsibility for the world's evolution to the point of maturity.

Hildegard herself was quite overwhelmed by this particular insight into the world and humanity as only a mirror-image of the immense totality of divine harmonies and by her simultaneous realization that even that vastness of the universe was but a reflection of the Deity himself: "Look again at the nature of humankind and see what you are! A human being already possesses heaven and earth and all creation in himself or herself. He or she is only a figure and form, yet one that conceals the whole universe within itself," for "God and human beings are one like the soul and the body, since God created them after his own image and likeness. All things have shadows, and humans are God's shadows, the outward signs of his creation. Humans are obvious signs of almighty God in all his wonders. They are shadows because they have a beginning. But God has no beginning and no end. The heavenly harmony reflects the Godhead and human beings reflect all the wonders of God" (CaCu 2, 17-19).

Physical beauty

"God has adorned the universe with glory and beauty. He has filled it to overflowing with the riches of creation, for the service of humankind" (LVM III, 26). The light of the Godhead illumines humans so that they appear in all their beauty and perfection of form (*plena statura*) and in all the shapeliness of their bodies (*opus corporis*).

At one time all the physical matter of the human body was light. The body was illuminated, penetrating, radiant and luminous in the *lumen corporis* (physical light) of its *genitura mystica* (mystical origin) and *natura gloriosa* (natural glory). This light was expressed in manifold hues and tints, limited only by the material confines of things but also enriching them, and therefore itself enhanced by the changes it brought about in their appearance. All aspects of the body were fire and incandescence, which became gleam and ardour in its eyes, a subdued glow in its limbs, a furious blaze within the caverns and enclosures of its entrails, and prophetic intensity in the dream-life of its visionary faculty.

If the light faded, sickness ensued. Death itself is the body with its light extinguished,

when the soul has long abandoned it like a fragment of burnt wood from which the fire can no longer draw the least flame. All life is a fiery culinary process, a single unique procedure of preparation and development.

The elementary substances of the world as a whole are cooked on the fire. The wind and the stars regulate the intensity of the process. The fiery soul bursts into flame in the body and ensouls the fruit like a ball of fire, then dwells in the limbs and bakes all the body's substances, finally consolidating their shape like pots in an oven. The soul flames roundabout the elements, attracts them, gets to know them, and starts talking to them—as it were. Everything in the world makes its contribution to this fiery elemental symphony, striving for consonance, the concordance of all living things, and thus ultimate harmony.

Adam and Eve were involved in a similar culinary process when they made love and came together as one flesh. They prepared and "cooked" one another, so that their substances were interfused. Just as the fruit of the human body is baked in the fire, so the Virgin

Mary was subject to the Holy Spirit brooding like a hen on its egg, and in this glowing process of divine gestation God became human. For Hildegard, cooking, baking, the action of fire, is a metaphor for life in the Spirit. Similarly, she sees her own piety as an evergreen substance maturing by God's grace in a fiery process until it emerges as a rich enunciation of truth: as "the flowering of divine beauty" and as the "adornment of his male power" (LVM IV, 28).

Only mature and sensitive human beings are in a position to appreciate the beauty of all earthly phenomena in their splendour (*splendere*), glory (*resplendere*), and radiant power. They become aware of the full beauty of nature and achieve an open view of the world. Nature as a whole is a single voice, with one tonality and sound of being (*sonus*) that makes the beauty of the world audible, visible, and comprehensible. Thus the earth appears as the "blossoming of divine beauty." All the works of God are resplendent with loveliness, and his cosmic order shines forth in the beauty of the world.

Accordingly, we should contemplate

"the sun, the moon and the stars and all the beauty of this life-giving natural greenness," and consider "the good fortune and happiness that God has bestowed on human beings in all these things" (LVM V, 16). Hildegard is never content with the mere appearance of beauty, with what we think is beautiful. She always goes to the source, to the things unknown from which these shapes are bodied forth, to the light by which these impressions are informed. Her visionary impulse is stilled only when she reaches that source, the mysteriously magnetic inner core of beauty itself. Then her quest turns into a search for a fitting response—for the right means of reflecting the extraordinary varieties of external nature, the beauty of fields and countryside, the nobility of mountains, the grandeur of gulfs and ravines, the vitality of roots and flowers, the fruitfulness of species, the splendour of the waters as they ebb and flow, the luminosity of the stars, the brilliant artistry with which the world enacts the drama of salvation, and then, of course, human beauty, which is the ultimate mirror of all these glories.

The gift of "happy

knowledge" (*laeta scientia*) enables human beings to perceive the mysteries of God's beautiful works (LDO V, 23) in and together with the world as a whole, and also to apprehend their own potential. They are able to enjoy a "happy life" (*vita laeta*). It is this same happiness that allows Hildegard to record the acknowledgement: "How beautiful your eyes are when you proclaim the works of the Lord!" (Sc III, 1).

Most beautiful of all, however (Hildegard tells us), are the faces of virgins in the early morning light, when they look up to contemplate their God. And God, she says, has enclosed all the beauty of heaven in the Virgin's womb (Sc III, 13). God himself looked at the "most beautiful of all human creatures" as the eagle directs his gaze to the sun (S 59). Just as the body mediates the world, intensifies life, and effectively symbolizes or "bodies forth" the Spirit, so the beautiful body becomes the medium for the planned transformation of the Word into human form and flesh. In this way Mary, the most beautiful and loveliest of beings, became the "mother of all joys." Her womb rejoiced when it resounded with the full symphony of heaven.

Here Hildegard's vision becomes a veritable mystical theology of beauty: God's glory has become flesh, and we have seen his beauty; for we have touched the Bread of Life with our hands and tasted it with our mouths. The Jesus she shows us here is not the suffering God-man who has "no form nor comeliness, nor beauty." He is not even the "delectable bridegroom of the soul," but the most beautiful of human beings, the very image and essence of beauty. Moreover, as the most beautiful of all beings, Hildegard's Jesus is most certainly a tender lover, yet also the "strongest lion" (*fortissimus leo*), who has "leapt from heaven to reside in the Virgin's chamber (*in aula virginis*)" (S 197). For Hildegard's Jesus is the cosmic Christ in whom time is centred and history culminates, the Lord of the cosmos who is making ready for the everlasting wedding feast. We too are adorned for the occasion, for we are resplendent in the clothing of the human form and already constitute, here on earth, "the members of his beautiful body (*membra sui pulchri corporis*)."

Hildegard presents this life as manifestly glorious and beautiful in all its physical reality because it issues from the unfathomable depths of God and because its meaning and mystery are centred in the incarnation of God. The body in all its sensuality is beautiful because in it we glimpse the door that opens onto the infinitely mysterious beauty of God. There is no evidence in later scholastic thinkers of this ungrudging and joyful acceptance of our own existence in all its fragility. They tended to play down and even to ignore the importance of the body. They overemphasized the soul instead, thus initiating one of the darker chapters not only of the "dark Middle Ages" but of seemingly enlightened "modern times."

At the end of the ages, however, human bodies will shine forth in all their beauty (LDO X, 1). Then our souls will be clothed "in that beauty which Adam lost and which they will now have restored to them not as it was but enhanced a thousandfold" (LVM VI, 55). The soul can reach the perfection of the Spirit only in union with the body. Consequently our souls "urgently desire to be sealed by their bodies, like hungry children asking their father for a crust of bread" (LVM II, 45). But, when time has reached its end, they will enjoy "the full health and wholeness of their bodies," taste the "most delightful of all pleasures, and rejoice in beauty unutterably radiant and splendid" (LVM VI, 58).

Human beings are at the centre of the world's structure, and are more important than all other creatures that depend on it. People may be small in stature, but their souls make them powerful. They have their heads erect and their feet on firm ground, and this dual ability to think and act enables them to control and accomplish both higher and lower things. The effects of what they do with their right and left hands are felt throughout the universe, because their inner power makes it possible for them to exploit its potential. Just as the human body is larger than the heart, so the soul's powers are stronger than the body's. Just as the human heart is concealed in the body, so the body is surrounded by the powers of the soul, which reach out over the whole world. Righteous people live in awareness of God and see him in all his works.

(LDO II, 15)

40. **The Ruler of the Universe**
A great golden-red circle of light emanates from God the Creator on his throne.

It surrounds the whole creation and illuminates the entire history of salvation.

Liber Scivias, copy of the former Rupertsberg Codex, *c.* 1180; St Hildegard's Abbey, Eibingen

41. **Universal Forces**
The universal wheel begins to turn about cosmic humanity—deprived of its divine background after the Fall. The wheel is driven by winds and animal impulses that keep everything in restless motion and also exert unhealthy influences on the human system of essential saps and juices.
Liber Divinorum Operum, *c.* 1240; Ms, 1942, Lucca, Biblioteca Statale.

The wheel of history

Human beings, so Hildegard tells us, entered the world in the context of a creation brought about in living light. Cosmic humanity appeared on the stage of a self-fulfilling historical drama every act of which proved to have cosmic implications. The overthrow of the first angel led to a cosmic catastrophe. The universal wheel began to turn and history started its calamitous course. Yet in the fullness of time Christ, the Son of the cosmos, appeared to restore order. Now the Church as the bride of God constructs its "Golden City" and shapes a new community of the future: a new earth and a new heaven.

Both the eternal, unsearchable counsel of God and the elucidation of the world's mystery face us, enclosed in a perpetual cycle. The material universe impinges on the temporal cosmos, where it searches for meaning and purpose. And there we find the representative human being, charged with the task of responsible decision on his or her own behalf.

The universal sphere is still held fast in the hands of the threefold Godhead. God reinforced this world with the winds, illuminated it with the stars, and allied it with the earth, because he wanted to use the earth's material to make the form with which he would become human. God has endowed human beings with all the world's substances and has given them the gift of reason to ensure that the whole world is at their disposal and that they can make creative use of it. He has given them access to human wholeness and redemption by offering them the possibility of a free decision made within the bounds of history.

Now the first decision has been made. The wheel of the world has been released and starts to turn. History begins its fateful course. The universal wheel, freed from its divine background, driven round and round by the winds and by animal impulses, persists in restless motion as it urges time ever onward. Borne on the winds, cosmic forces enter the system of human sap and juices, introduce disorder and sickness into the human organism, and thus affect the moral behaviour of humankind. The basic equilibrium of the fluids and forces of the human system is disturbed. People become sick and are forced to live in an alien environment. They leave their original life of health and joy and enter a period of exile and homelessness. They are no longer people as they were intended to be—purely and simply human.

Yet these fallen creatures come to themselves, face the world anew, and commit themselves to all the creatures and things that surround them, searching for the wholeness which they hope to recreate in conjunction with the entire created world. Therefore God allows people to move on a circular path and to follow their own course like wheels turning within the spiritual environment of their lives (*ut rotam in spiritu vitae circuire*). He allows us to proceed on our own way yet always calls us home, for he is always mysteriously at work in all things (*omnia comprehendit, quoniam operatus est*).

The symbol of history is the image of the *rota*, the great universal wheel of the constant cycle of time. We move through the cosmic order as if through a palpable landscape. And once the whole realm of space has been traversed, time, the *opus temporum* (LDO IV, 98), becomes the scene of action. Everything in time as in nature takes on a profound symbolic meaning, for everything has its part to play in a single vast cosmic liturgy and in the ultimate cosmic mystery of the Incarnation.

Two central images constantly recur in Hildegard's visions: the work (*opus*) and the word (*verbum*). God's Word is at work in the world. The structure of the cosmos, which is nature, mysteriously affects the course taken by the world, which is its history. In their lifetime, human beings have to elucidate both realms, that of outer and that of inner reality, and they are responsible for both, for history and for nature. The image of "labour" unites both key-terms of the new age: "nature" and "work." The full unity of creation—in angels, plants, and animals, in the life of the senses, and in the striving of the soul or mind—may reveal the intended results of the creation's glorification of its sole Maker, but also how human beings manage only to subsist or even fail in their everyday *operatio* (functioning).

This idea of the world comprises all natural, but also all cultural and historical phenomena. In both areas we experience the numinous as well as the delightful aspects of God's actions, of his reality. Hildegard as prophetess and visionary saw and felt the numinous quality of everything in her natural environment: fire and water, clouds and streams, the sun and the stars, winds and storms, the moon and the night, a spring, a meadow, the flowers and the miraculously never-failing greenness of the life-force, with all the varieties of growth, sprouting and blossoming.

Hildegard was certainly a child of nature, but she was also captivated by cultural phenomena: by the cultivation and harvesting of fields; the building of houses and monasteries; the shape of a vessel and the work of artists; the devices and achievements of human activity in the world and the threats posed to them by inadequacy and failure, the anxiety and anguish of guilt, and the bottomless pit of sin; and, day after day, hour after hour, the unavoidable necessity of human decision-making in the midst of all this action.

Hildegard experienced both realms of existence as a unity, as the one indivisible reality (*unum opus*). She did not so to speak downgrade effort and achievement or even demonize ineptitude and collapse while treating stars, stones, plants, and animals as inspired and spiritual entities. She saw everything as comprising and serving only the fundamental experience of the one unique human reality, for we know no other.

For Hildegard, mature people enjoy the full potential of their creative power and the summertime of their lives. Like the sun, they are granted power over time and can regulate the pace of life. Everything makes its appearance in accord with the rhythm of time: the rapidity of light as it arrives and the predictability of its fading; the compulsion of growth; the evidence of plants budding; the density of natural greenness; the withering and decay of what was once fresh and verdant; all metamorphoses and twilight moments; and even the mysterious transforming action of nightfall. For Hildegard, this kind of experiential wisdom is self-evidently necessary in a world where the sun and the moon wax and wane, human beings have to eat and defecate, sleep and wake up, grow and die. But she realizes that all this takes place in a world where they must expect suffering as well as hope, knowledge and happiness.

Originally constituted (*constitutio prima*) to enjoy an edenic existence in health and wholeness (*genitura mystica*), humans were entrusted with a virtually universal cultural responsibility for the world (*opus cum creatura*). All the elements of the world served human beings, and all creatures were available for their cooperation and use. Breathing in and out were symbolic of a cosmic concordance of all that was. Eating and drinking served the purposes of interaction with the world and not those of mere sustenance for the day-by-day maintenance of existence. Sleeping and waking were the media of a prophetic understanding of the world and not a means of reviving the body. Even sexual activity was the most profound expression of personal harmony and integration, the means of intimate self-development in and with another person (*opus alterum per alterum*).

The first figure in history to emerge from the creative hands of God was Adam, the first human being, whom God placed in the resplendent light of paradise. "He was immaculately beautiful and dwelled in a bright country." A brilliant white cloud projected from his side and carried the whole human race like dazzling stars within its womblike interior. God held his work in an embrace of unequalled love. "How exceedingly beautiful was the form that God bestowed on this man moulded from the earth's clay!"

God wanted to give Adam another being of the same nature to whom he would cleave and who would cleave to him in mutual address and response. With the creation of woman, dramatic tension entered into human history.

42. **The Works of the Six Days of Creation**
Once the six days' work is complete, the glowing white flame is concen- *trated on a lump of clay from which a live human being begins to emerge.* Detail from "Creation and Redemption"

Liber Scivias, copy of the former Rupertsberg Codex, *c.* 1180; St Hildegard's Abbey, Eibingen

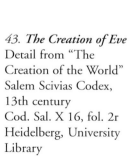

*43. **The Creation of Eve***
Detail from "The
Creation of the World"
Salem Scivias Codex,
13th century
Cod. Sal. X 16, fol. 2r
Heidelberg, University
Library

*44. **Summer Landscape***
Carmina Burana,
early 13th century
Col. 4550, fol. 64v
Munich, Bavarian State
Library

88

Woman's role in the history of salvation

With the unique enthusiasm of a profoundly visionary artist the Lord God carried out the fundamental act of generation and made Paradise the site of all forms of loveliness, vitality, and harmonious growth. The whole earth was designed as a single garden of love tilled only by modesty and resounding with joyful melodies.

When God made Adam, Adam received a great gift of love, which God bestowed on him while he was sleeping. "And God gave the man's love a form, and the man's love was woman" (CaCu 136, 18-20). This was the "guiltless Eve," of whom Adam had dreamed in all innocence. "Now she would dwell with him in the garden of delights. She carried all the children of humankind as brilliant lights in her womb" (Sc I, 2). This happened while Adam was asleep, in a state of something akin to mystical contemplation during which his impulse to love became so compelling that sheer desire evoked a physical response.

This process of demand and response produced the clear outlines of the human being: man *and* woman. Each rejoices in the other and achieves ultimate self-expression and perfect development in and with the other, in a life of perfect love in the garden of loving delight. In the mystery of being human, people still trace out the path to their intended dwelling-place, recognizing present signs of their intended glory. Their joy now is a kind of sublime nostalgia for a former state of existence, but for one that could be restored. The way they follow has its joys, but it can also be the way of the cross. Yet the human race is also the physical centre and point of unity in spite of all division and contention. Human life is a constant testing-ground where in times of need and trial we are fortified by memories of paradise and encouraged by signposts to our everlasting home. Nostalgia is a tiny spring from the great source of love that will open out into the happiness of eternity.

Here we have the first mention of the main topic of salvation history (which will be discussed fully in the chapter on "Creation and redemption"). The conversation between the Creator and his creation is to be conducted as an "interchange between lovers," in devoted "warmth and harmony." God has adorned his creatures with his greatest possible gift of love, for he himself has become human. God has become a human being "just as the bridegroom receives his bride into the love-nest of his heart, so that there, in the fullness of his love, he can present her with all the treasures of his heart" (LVM 1V, 32). In all behaviour on the part of creation that may be described as service there is an ineradicable "longing for the Creator's kiss, for the whole world accepted its Creator's embrace when God gave it all that it could possibly require" (LVM V, 39).

Once again Hildegard describes the special part played by women in the history of salvation when she proclaims the message of wisdom in the imagined words of Solomon: "But I would compare the Creator's great love for his creation and that of creation for its Creator with the love and trust with which God joined man and woman in a single union, so that they themselves might be fruitful and creative in their turn. Just as all creation issued from God, so it remains dependent on God, stays attached to him, and does nothing without his command. In the same way a woman looks to her man to answer his call to her in mutual joy and response. The creation gives its Creator a special sign of attachment by serving him in all its undertakings. But the Creator is united with his creation when he gives it the reviving freshness of life and the force of fruitful vitality. The world would be enveloped in total darkness if it withdrew from its union with God and abandoned any of its commitments. But it prospers and flowers as long as it acknowledges its responsibilities. Only thus can life be lived with due order and be said to be of good repute, when all needs are taken properly into account and are duly satisfied" (LVM V, 39).

Therefore the creation too should respond to its Creator in loving intimacy, as if to a Lover. It should desire a true resting-place at the end of history: its natural home where, when the ages have reached their culminating-point, God of his infinite goodness will finally satisfy all its needs.

In the light of the seasons

In the Hildegardian scheme of things, God has exemplified the whole of nature in human beings. In the ways proper to humanity, therefore, they depict nature and predict history. They not only mirror, say, the seasons of the year but foreshadow the drama of history, which is also reflected in the glass of daily life. The practical results of human action in the world emerge and their consequences are experienced not in some kind of isolation, but in accordance with the course of nature and with the progression of the months of the year. What we think of as nature in one major sense, the verdant earth, lies at the very heart of creation; it is the home and creative space of humankind. Nature and history are essential factors in deciding what human beings will be like. Furthermore, the parts these determining elements play in the events of salvation history have a crucial effect on the reconciliation of the Creator with his creation.

Accordingly, the year is portrayed as a sphere replete with all the features of nature. It symbolizes all forms of activity and progression: the earth's character, its heat and cold; waxing and waning light; the gamut of colours and the vital, fundamental greenness that is cultivated and baked until it becomes golden-brown ripeness; the human body and its various organs corresponding to the divisions of the world; and the five senses of the soul, which apprehend the meaning of the planets and ascertain the world's decypherable actuality and potential. Hildegard represents all this as a living and mysteriously rhythmic whole.

Every aspect of this everyday rhythm of existence needs symbols and signs to be appreciated proficiently. It seeks a palpable order in terms of, say, daily mealtimes, as well as in the constant round of sleeping and waking, movement and rest. The months of the year accord with the nature and progression of the heavens, as with the course of human life: with birth and nurture, with maturation and crises, with growing old and dying.

The rich visual imagery of the Lucca Codex of Hildegard's *Book of Divine Works* displays the very pulse of life as bound up with the practical sequence of seasonal tasks: trees are felled, the ground is prepared, and ripe fruit is gathered. Game is hunted, hay is taken in, corn is cut, and the harvest is brought home. Then people rest and celebrate.

Here the seasons are not shown in conformity with the traditional division into spring, summer, autumn, and winter. Instead they are represented as a set of dualisms: as a complex of contrasted pairs of basic properties such as "hot and dry" or "cold and wet." Evidently, Hildegard was not interested in such tropes as the tender lyricism of spring or the anticipated melancholy of autumn. Nor did she concern herself with Easter rejoicing or Whitsun celebrations, with May devotions or All Souls' commemorations; and there is no trace in her works of anything like Advent expectation or of Christmas as a major seasonal feast.

The earliest months stand for purging and purification, for putting things right. The "eye of conscience" ensures that the immature human being is kept free from all possible taint. The ensuing months are the time of confrontation between humanity and the gathering, stirring forces of nature—the tempestuous impulses that arise in the "full flush of youth." The fourth month is full of vigorous life and enchanting fragrance; its symbol is the nose, the organ of contact and of keeping a judicious distance, which also stands for the wisdom that resides "as a sweet scent of order in all works of art." May brings sight or the "sense of the eyes," which "rejoices the human heart" and makes everything evident, conceivable, and apprehensible. Sight enables us to discern things and to discriminate between them by means of our reason, which is the "spine, bones, and marrow supporting and sustaining the five senses." The summer months announce the ripeness of nature and the perspicacity of the increasingly alert and mature human being. Now the faculty of inward hearing becomes apparent as the commencement of the rational soul or true intellect. Now humans are "efficiently selective beings," and really able to decide whether things taste right and to judge them accordingly. Finally, with the full development of the sense of touch, people have an effective yardstick for assessing

The natural world

Hildegard's picture of the world shows us nature in all its ripe maturity. It is a realm replete with signs and symbols, which we encounter directly in stones and stars, plants and animals, in all the basic forces, and in the Word itself. "All elements served human beings voluntarily because they saw that humans possessed life. They cooperated with their enterprises and worked with them, as humans did with them. In consideration of this reciprocal agreement, the earth offered people its vitality (*viriditas*), in accordance with human nature and character and in conformity with the operation of the human mind and the course of their life-cycle" (PL 1125). Human beings are so to speak the bright green heart of the vital plenitude of nature. Their heart is the gateway to the world. Accordingly the heart also leads to all the elements of existence, "by means of which people enact and achieve what the life-force within them impels them to do" (CaCu 96, 10/11).

Hildegard calls all the elements of the world, together with their corresponding forces in the systems of the winds and air-currents and in the star-laden realms of space, the "firmament." The firmament is the cosmic base-plate and universal supportive structure. But we should not conceive of this universal construction as something static. On the contrary, it is always in dynamic motion, on its way toward perfection. It is secured, but in fire; it moves through the air; it is drenched in water; it is illuminated by the stars; and it is supported by the winds. Each of these spheres is intimately related to all the others and to the whole. None of them can take effect alone and of itself. Each of them exists in a state of reciprocal tension and in a condition of demand and response, and must act responsibly by taking the whole into account. The world is a universal structure, an orderly network in which everything must correspond and react appropriately. Consequently there is a relationship of interactivity between all creatures (*creatura per creaturam continetur*). The whole world exists in a cosmic partnership just as human beings have to exist sociologically; that is, in a network of fellowship.

Therefore each part of the whole has its appropriate path or cycle, and no one part should trespass on the particular course of any other. Thus the "pure ether" must withstand the mortal miasma or deadly fog that emanates from what Hildegard calls "black fire," in order to dry everything green on the earth and remove the moisture from the fields. The "tender air" has to make the earth fruitful by "tempering" it, and thus ensuring a proper equilibrium of properties. Even the most extreme "flaming fire" has to course through all the spheres of the earth in order to contribute the gleam of beauty proper to everything natural, and, indeed, to even the most obscure corner and object on this earth. Just as flame issues from fire and brilliance is a quality of flame, so the beauty of heaven and earth shine out from the deepest mysteries of fire. Fire, after all, is the essential matter of every gleam of beauty.

But this world is inscribed in the human body itself. All the elements of the world were created for humanity and are there ready to serve people. "For God established the universal order of things and equipped it with the elements."

"God has adorned the universe with brilliance and beauty. He has filled it with the riches of creation, for the service of humankind" (LVM III, 26). Everything that lives on earth "has a fundamental urge to embrace some other in love. All nature is available to humanity and willingly offers people its benefits in loving service" (LVM I, 17).

The meaning and direction of the whole

47. The Source of Life
In pre-modern times, water was the symbol of life in all developed cultures throughout the world. In the Christian West it also came to stand for salvation. Outer purification always assists inner sanctification. Human beings are intended to bathe in the spiritual waters, the depths of the spring of life and the source from which the whole creation draws its greatest beauty and rich vitality. The book of nature holds a universal literature, an entire cosmic alphabet, ready for us to decypher.
Charlemagne's Gospels (Godescal Gospels), 781-783
Paris, Bibliothèque Nationale

48. The Universe
The earth, the human home, lies at the centre of creation. The universe is illuminated by stars and planets, refreshed by winds, and enclosed in fire that stands for God's all-embracing love.

Liber Scivias, copy of the former Rupertsberg Codex, *c.* 1180; St Hildegard's Abbey, Eibingen

creation are evident in this setting of useful order and supportive moderation. Every creature has its proper place and fulfils its due function. Nothing suffers from any kind of deprivation, and nowhere is there any trace of imbalance or excess. That is the proper state of the works of God (*operatio Dei*). But the essential, central work of all this divine activity is humanity (*opus operis Dei*). Therefore all the laws of the universe and all the forces of nature have to be interpreted in human terms. The fundamental structure of the cosmos is anthropocentric.

Accordingly, everything in the divine order is action and reaction, address and response: "The stars sparkle with the moon's light and the moon is illuminated by the sun's fire. Each thing serves something higher and nothing exceeds its due measure" (LVM II, 22). Located as they are in this universal order, human beings learn to see God really, just as God really expects us to make our proper showing in all these things. The whole world is intended to disclose itself naturally to humanity, so that people can use and cooperate with its elementary forces, for humans could never live and persist in living without the basic structure of nature (LDO II, 2). "Consequently, humanity is entirely the full work of God (*plenum opus Dei*). Only humans know, survey and control the requirements of the earth and discern heavenly things in the mirror of faith" (LDO IV, 92).

God himself, the "great Architect of the world," made it possible for his work, human beings, to "perform their actions so that, by means of earth, water, air, and fire (of which, after all, they themselves are composed), they might bring all God's and their own works to fruition" (LVM VI, 59). Accordingly, "nowhere in the entire world is there any creature without any light of its own, whether greenness or seed, flowers or beauty, for otherwise it would not be something created by God" (LDO IV, 11). The absolute essential truth of things in this world is reflected in the state of just being beautiful. This is one of the key notions in Hildegard's wholly optimistic view of the world.

Even in nature in a withered, atrophied state, Hildegard sees the mysterious workshop of creativity, where everything is waiting, quite prepared and absolutely alive and intending to burst forth, but now weaving and working at

its intention. The summer is flowering, maturing wakefulness. Similarly, the winter is restful sleep and restoration of strength. Like sleep, winter is not a dead phase but in fact the really active one. In winter all the rich heat of the sun is taken into an inward, intimate sphere, just as in sleep the marrow is cooked through thoroughly and thus intensified with new potential, so that it can provide the new day with renewed power. All this, says Hildegard, is sensible and beautiful: "The valleys turn green and soon flower with the dew of heaven and the sun's heat, but not so long after they dry out and fade as tempestuous seasons arrive." But the Lord God has not forgotten even these valleys, even though at times they lose their beauty, for they do so only to rise again soon in all their beauty (PL 368 C).

The original planting of God's lovely garden is discernible in nature if we see it in this way. If we look at things in the right light we can see God's presence in creation, that flowering "garden in which the Lord delights and feasts his eyes." The creation is also a feast for our eyes, for us who should contemplate in wonder and delight all that we can read in the book of nature while we decipher the meaning of every symbol and sign (*vestigia*), conversing with all things just as we ourselves are addressed and learning to know the meaning and quality of the nature entrusted to us fallen humans. For it shares our fate, points out our melancholy condition even as it mourns over it, but also demonstrates the reasons for our hope that one day we shall be restored to our true home with the Creator of all things. For the spiritual purpose of all nature is to be God's dwelling-place in creation.

Of course, since the fall of the first human being, our former, utterly automatic and reliable, healthy interaction with nature has been out of joint. Now humans lead a life of care and anxiety. They become sick and make others and things unhealthy, because their activity is ill-judged and unfaithful to the Word. They have failed in their original mission and commission and have become rebels (*homo rebellis*) in the midst of creation.

In their fallen and alienated state, human beings also caused external nature to fall into a state of confusion. Furthermore, they displaced the workings of time and distorted its movement. This was the start of the great

*49. The Universe with
the Four Elements and
the Four Winds*
Cod. 2582, f. 237r
Vienna, Austrian
National Library

99

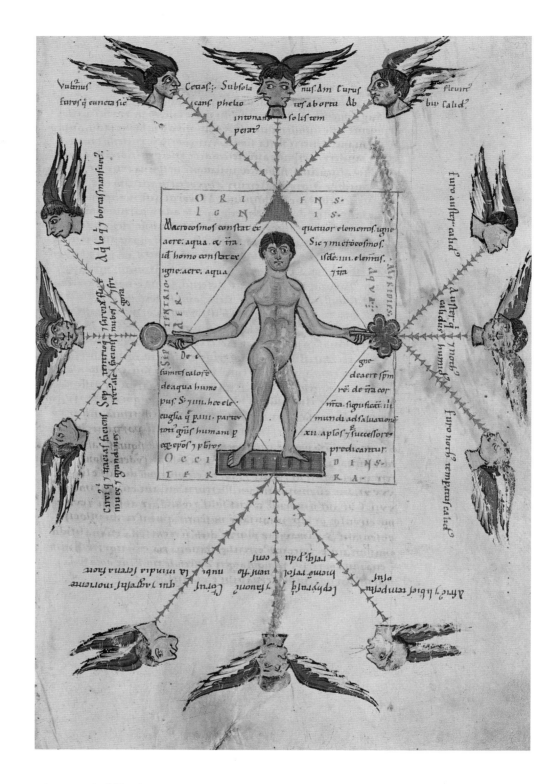

*50. The Human Micro-
cosm with the Four
Elements and the Winds*
Prüfening, 3rd quarter
of the 12th century

Astronomical Treatises,
Cod. 12600, fol. 29r
Vienna, Austrian
National Library

100

cosmic catastrophe. The firmament began to turn in an attempt to cleanse its soiled elements. Since then time has turned and turned, urging itself onward to ultimate correction and redemption in the course of history, so that the world can be saved and nature, always sighing in the misery of its discontent, can be assuaged and redeemed. "If people only behaved as they were originally intended to behave (in accordance with their *constitutio prima*) then all the times and climates of the year would be the same. One springtime would be like any other, and this summer would turn out just like any other, and so on. But because people in their disobedience neglected the respect and love they owed to God the elements and the seasons alike now overstep their natural bounds" (CaCu 17, 21-27).

The elements cry out in complaint "and, together with the rest of creation, accuse humanity of having allowed its despicable nature (*vilis natura*) to rebel so appallingly against God within so short a existence, whereas the other creatures continue to obey his commandments in honour and respect. Accordingly, the elements shout their complaints at human behaviour and raise their voices in fear and outrage" (Sc III, 5).

The frightening "lamentation of the elements" (*querula elementorum*) is clear and unmistakable: "We can no longer keep going as before and complete our natural course as intended. For humans twist, crunch, and grind us as in a mill, from top to bottom. We, the elements—the winds and the waters—stink to high heaven, like the plague itself. We are almost starving from hunger for true equilibrium" (LVM III, 2).

This lament is answered by the "Man of God" (*Vir Deus*): "I shall sweep you clean with my broom and pursue these humans until they repent and come home again. But all the winds are still full of mildew and mould, and the air spews out so much filth that people hardly dare open their mouths lest they breathe in all this pollution." Humans have sinned against the earth. "They have fouled the air and dimmed the light with all this pestilential filth (*foeditas et pestilentia*)." Just as the creation as a whole was summoned to serve humanity, it is now quite contrary to human needs. It is in opposition; it is nature in a state of need and demand. Everything

external to humans has been forced into a state of rebellion, for it has been carried along by human revolt, and has been upset by human restlessness and confusion (*inquietudo*) until it allows terrible things (*horribiles terrores*) to happen (LVM III, 43).

In the original state and constitution (*constitutio*) of humanity God set human beings down as a constituent part of a wholesome and healthy earth. They are intended to enjoy a happy life (*vita laeta*) in this world as their proper home and environment. As a result of falling into sin (*destitutio*) human beings were displaced and alienated from their proper surroundings. Now they are out of true with the world. They are uprooted and divided. People wander through nature and its beauties full of homesickness and nostalgia for what was and might be again. But God invites them home again out of his loving grace and will restore them in his goodness. In that sure conviction people can now work enthusiastically to restore the world by building a new one (*restitutio*), so that ultimately they can live a full physical existence in the fullness of joy and in the love of God. For love is the "home and fortress of divine mystery."

In our relations with nature we live in hope of health and redemption, for nature as such bears the impression of God's own masterstamp. In this respect we come to understand that God is not something wholly other and alien, cold destiny, the unmerciful law of nature, or just harsh fate. The world is coloured with promise. Human beings are able to reason and divine something other and better than the human condition. Their spirit is an organ of healing. God still dwells with us in the Word that already existed in the beginning and became Man in our own human history. He lives here with us but longs to take us home with him to the blessed marriage-feast.

Nature nevertheless remains the beautiful, vast, mighty world with all its plants and animals. It is a world that was originally blessed and sanctified, even though set awry by human sin, and its vocation is still to dwell with human beings in a cosmos transfigured in glory. The world offers human beings a wealth of phenomena and images that declare all this to be the case. God made all creatures for humans to look at and understand (LDO V, 34) and so that people could read the truth of the Spirit in the lines of nature, where he has

51. The Fall
The fallen man lies at right-angles to creation with one ear open to the powers of darkness. Eve, depicted as a white cloud bearing the whole human race like so many stars in her womb, emerges from his side. The four elements are in a state of unhealthy confusion at the four corners of the picture. But the Garden of Eden with its trees and plants is not closed to human beings.

Liber Scivias, copy of the former Rupertsberg Codex, *c.* 1180; St Hildegard's Abbey, Eibingen

102

inscribed them so unmistakably. Nature was entrusted to us, and we come to know and understand ourselves by acquainting ourselves with it and by interpreting and comprehending it. In everything phenomenal there outside us we experience exactly the same profound mysteries that we come to know as our essential destiny in the intimacy of our own soul. It is all one and the same reality: nature with all its riches, indeed the entire universe, is there to illuminate, explain, and complete—in short, to enlighten—our existence.

The four elements in humankind

Fire, earth, water, and air. These four elements are at the very centre of human beings. They are their basic constitution: "Fire gives them heat, air allows them breath, water offers them blood, and earth endows them with firm tissue." Or, as Hildegard also puts it: "Fire gives them sight, air allows them hearing, water offers them motion, and the earth endows them with their upright posture. Throughout the world everything thrives in succulence and abundance when the elements perform their tasks properly, so that heat, dew, and rain descend exactly as each should, at the due times and to the extent called for; so that the earth and its fruits are nurtured carefully, and effective fruitfulness and health are the assured results" (CaCu 49/50).

This absolutely fundamental physical system is directly related to the basic forces of the universe. It is also intimately associated with the economy and equilibrium of body and mind and with a life of grace. The feet are live rivers, for they carry people through the cycle of their existence. The nose is like the realms of the atmosphere: it symbolizes the order of nature as well as that of culture. As an organ of wisdom it helps us to orientate ourselves and to adjust our sense of distance. Universal space may also be thought of as a kind of gigantic stomach, with an input and output that mirror our own existential dependence on the world without.

Hildegard offers us another, actually very lucid metaphor when she cites the four elements in connection with the powers of the different virtues. First there is the earth, which holds everything in embryonic form deep within itself, and is the source of all the vitality that produces blossom and flower. It is so to speak the flowering and beauty of God's male potency (LVM IV, 28). This potency, or *Vir Deus*, is glorified in and through the earth because the earth supplies the material for what God does in and through humanity; and humanity in its turn provides the material for the Incarnation of the Son of God (LVM IV, 29).

The earth's powers take effect in the human organism in many different ways: in growth as the vital life-giving force (*viriditas*); in the capacity of fading and withering purposively (*ariditas*); in generation as the capability of production (*vivificatio*); and in the dutiful cooperation of all organs in an especially intimate and compassionate relationship with human beings. Hildegard adds the supremely meaningful key to these inevitably earthly and earthy images of sky and earth, body and soul, man and woman, when she depicts this earth's ultimate mystery as something over and above them all: the mystery of its essential radiant density: "All forms of earthly creation are formed from the earth. For this motherly earth of ours (*materna terra*) is the basic material (*materia*) of God's work for humanity: and that is the Incarnation of the Son of God" (LVM IV, 1).

Human beings are also sustained by fire. In their fiery substance they "are so to speak the light of the rest of creation, a source of illumination for everything that dwells with them on earth" (LDO IV, 17). This essential flame or ardency of humanity gives us all good things, arouses all goodness, and inspires all goodness. It is the foundation on which holiness erects its great building, which towers through the atmosphere into the infinite heights above. Similarly, the gentle fragrant breath of life's green freshness impels our longing for the Bread of Life ever onward, to ever greater heights (LVM VI, 21/22).

Finally, with the many thousandfold powers of water, the Spirit offers us heat, dissolves the curdled and congealed residues of sin, and with the overflowing rivers of truth urges everything toward a spiritual dimension. It removes fur from arteries and opens up blocked ducts, until "in the vitalizing onrush of profound sorrow and tears that then becomes a flood it pours out the juice of contrition and flushes the hardened human

heart with repent-
ance." Then, together
with the birds, we rise
into the air; swim like
fishes in the water of
faith; wander over the
fields like animals; and
even creep and crawl
along the tracks of
humility like worms,
snails or reptiles. In
this way, together with
the whole of creation,
we are always advanc-
ing along the road to
ever-greater holiness
(LVM VI, 23).

Greenness brings forth the blossom, and the
blossom the fruit. Clouds travel across the
heavens. The moon and the stars burn in all
their brilliance and fiery energy. The life-force
urges new flowers from dry and withered
wood. Everything there is has an outward and
inward way of being: what is apparent and
what is concealed. We see only faint shadows; we do not perceive the mighty driving-
force behind all things, whose workings the
human mind labours to disclose and interpret
with all the resources of knowledge and
science. (PL 171 A).

Only humanity knows the Word, which is
the source of reason. God's Word impinges on
every aspect of the world and evokes a living
response wherever it is received. The Spirit
goes forth, vitalizes the world, and inspires
everything fruitful. This is the process which
we call life.

52. The Order of the
Four Elements
Detail from "Redemption"
Liber Scivias, copy of the
former Rupertsberg
Codex, *c.* 1180;
St Hildegard's Abbey,
Eibingen

56. Healing the Possessed
Gospels of Otto III.
Reichenau, late 10th
century
Cod., lat. Ms 4453
Munich, Bavarian
State Library

Hildegard's biographer describes the dramatic occasion when a certain possessed, or severely mentally distressed and unstable woman, Sigewiza from Brauweiler near Cologne, was apparently treated with exorcism or the ritual expulsion of demonic powers. Hildegard accepted this difficult case at the request of Abbot Gedolph of Brauweiler. To the dismay of her Sisters, after merely offering suitable advice on her treatment and finding that inadequate, in the end the abbess brought the woman to stay in the convent itself. There she tried out a kind of "group therapy" in order to cure the woman's disturbed state of mind. This communual treatment consisted of ensuring she was in a familiar space with supportive people, and that there were constant expressions of understanding and sympathy for her. The community supplemented these measures with almsgiving, ascetic practices, and prayer. The main therapeutic tool, however, was Hildegard's own series of conversations with the tormented woman, whose health was eventually restored (V 91-118). "We watched the diabolical aura weakening day by day until it finally disappeared. Thus this woman was freed from her suffering. She was restored to full strength of body and soul and enjoyed the best of health" (Bw 53/54)

Holistic healing

Hildegard's book on health, *Causae et curae*, also offers a complete system of holistic healing (*ratio sanationis*). She gives detailed prescriptions for infusions and compounds, poultices and compresses, fumigations, rinses and irrigations, powders and pills, and all kinds of medicines. At first sight, some now seem very quaint indeed. For instance, ants (*formica*) are the basis of several remedies she recommends. An ant bath, she says, is good for gout, and an ant ointment effective with leprosy. Someone who feels deeply depressed should take a cloth with ants on, and put it on his or her heart until sweating starts. This will soon produce a relieved mind (*suavis mens*) and a happy disposition (*laetus*). When the patient's head is entirely cleared of worries (*bonus intellectus*) he or she can get down to everyday tasks again (PL 1338 A). Hildegard also advises the use of spelt (*spelta*) as the best wheat because it is softer and kinder than other sorts. Spelt "makes you feel happy and brings joy to the human heart" (PL 1131 C/D).

Generally speaking, however, Hildegard in her healing art is concerned not so much with treatments that put things right (*restitutio ad integrum*) as with restoring people to a sensible and healthy way of life (*restitutio ad integritatem*). When concentrating on this point, she refers not so much to the means of curing people as to the powers and forces that help them to a cure: the curative powers of language, music, and relating personally to the sick individual. "After all," says Hildegard (who comes down quite heavily on physicians who "just mix up medicines"), "what is the point of offering a medicinal remedy if you don't add the tonic of your own virtue?"

These basic criteria are fundamental to the medieval understanding of physiology and pathology. For Hildegard and other proficient healers of her time, sickness is not merely a process but inadequacy and failure of intended purpose. Creative effort is possible only in a state of health. And that, for Hildegard, means the kind of health that draws creativity from the vital determining force of nature (*viriditas*).

Hildegard's healing art is a distinctive and successful synthesis of the *techne therapeutike* (practical therapy) of classical antiquity and the Christian spirit of *humanitas* (humanity) and *misericordia* (mercy or compassion). The proper attitude for a medical doctor or healer is not so much seeking an empirically demonstrable cure at any price but an expression and application of the *misericordia* that one human person is capable of and ready to show to another. Mercy is always directed to someone else (*flectens se ad hominem*), and the person who shows it suffers together with the afflicted person (*miseriis compatiens*). A compassionate individual behaves like the Good Samaritan (*imitans Samaritanum*), and just expresses his or her common humanity (*cooperiens hominem*) (Sc III, 3).

Only in the setting of such a relationship between fellow-humans can a sick person be truly acknowledged as who he or she really is. The patient needs recognition as this particular person with these specific traits. The poor and sick need our attention, Hildegard tells us, "because as humans they are our brothers and sisters." A sick person is closer to God because God can give meaning and purpose to his or her need and suffering. Hildegard was all the more effective a healer because she was able to recognize her own sickness and difficulties. "I am a poor creature lacking health, force, strength, and education," for I am "a mere shadow of vitality and health." Hildegard herself was indeed a *homo patiens*, a suffering human creature, but one whom *Christus Medicus*, Christ the physician, met, and treated. And Christ is the doctor qualified to treat all diseases, for "he is the great physician who keeps his patients alive and vigilant, shakes the sleeping soul into awareness, and only allows those to fall into the void who insist on maintaining their evil course."

"I am," Christ says, "the most competent specialist for all forms of disease, and I treat them like a doctor who sees a patient who really needs medicine" (Sc I, 3). Christ, therefore, is the model for all those whom God has called to guide, care for and heal people. They should imitate him by practising the virtues of discretion (*discretio*), mercy (*misercordia*), and justice (*justitia*). For all the works of God are a unique *symphonia*, a single song of praise for justice (LVM IV, 3).

Greenness

Hildegard of Bingen constantly refers to the fundamental creative power of the life-force as "greenness." This radiating green vitality (*viriditas*) shines through and from the structures of the world and in the juice of each single organism (*fulgens in opere hominis*). In this way it gives biological and cosmic forces a common purpose, bringing them into ethical consensus, as it were. The heavens and the earth and all its beauties are essentially products of this basic green vitality.

Initially, greenness (*viriditas*) is experienced quite naturally. We perceive it in a very basic way as the revivification, sprouting and blossoming of external nature. In this context we experience simply what growth and development, sprouting and flourishing mean if all goes well: they imply a strong and healthy life, or "essential greenness," to adopt Hildegard's term. In all the varieties and several beauties of the natural world we see a thousand different forms of greening in stalks and leaves. This greenness originates in the four elements: earth and fire, water and air. It is sustained by the four qualities: by dry and moist, by cold and hot. This green lives in fire, shimmers in water, moistens stone, and takes particularly refreshing effect in the atmosphere from which "the grasses in the early morning suck up their greenness as greedily as a lamb its milk" (PL 1249 B). Green is the light which, once it has been urged forth, thoroughly drenches and then bakes all things in this world in the sun's fire until their variegated colours and qualities reach the point of golden maturity.

A tree is a prime example of this process. The function performed by a tree's sap falls to the soul in a human body. Its powers or abilities enable it to unfold or develop its form just as the tree does. Its intelligence (*intellectus*) is like the green of branches and leaves; its will (*voluntas*) is like blossoming; its spirit (*animus*) is like the fruit in preparation; and its reason (*ratio*) like the fruit come to fruition or maturity. Finally, its good sense or purposive reason (*sensus*) is like the ultimate form of the tree extending and spreading out to its full height and width. Accordingly, in all these manifestations and expressions, the soul is "the body's inner framework and shaping support" (Sc I, 4).

Consequently, not only flesh and blood are green, but everything to do with the vitalizing power of the body that we might include in the concept of "soul." A woman becomes fruitful in the greenness of her blood, where her life-giving primordial impulse becomes evident (*viriditas floriditatis feminae*). Yet this greenness is only a reflection, a symbolic representation of the truly primordial vitality, the ultimately primal power, which lies hidden in the ground of eternity. This brilliant green spectrum of possibilities pours forth from the natural order, and grows ever denser and richer as it emanates from the glowing core of the fire of eternal life, from whose mysterious green depths it trickles into the embryonic forces of the cosmos, into the vital forces that empower and shape the generations of humanity, and into the "tender greenness" of the Incarnation.

"There is a power that has been since all eternity," says Hildegard, "and that force and potentiality is green!" It showed its might in Abraham. He was the father of all potency. It broke through and out in Christ when he forced the bounds of the heavens with a lion's strength in order to become human flesh in the Virgin's womb. Therefore Mary is known as the "greenest of virgins" (*viridissima virgo*). Wholeness and redemption entered the world from her tender-bright and luminous womb. She is the "bright Mother of the holy art of healing" (*mater sanctae medicinae*), since she was married to integrity, to the sound and healthy Whole, to very Health and saving Perfection whole and entire.

Accordingly, *viriditas* is the supremely illuminative principle of the natural driving-force, the life-force that is always purposively directed toward healing and wholeness. Love, too, is the breath of the same vital green power that sustains all life's greenness. The Holy Spirit gives human beings the green and open space where they are capable of responding in the Word, and of dedicating themselves of their own free will to the joint enterprise of creation. The Spirit purifies the world, scours away all guilt, and heals all wounds and sadness. The Spirit ignites and inspires us and everything as its makes its way through our

57. The Tree of Jesse
Salem Scivias Codex,
13th century
Cod. Sal. X 116, fol. 4r
Heidelberg, University
Library

horribly alienated reality; yet throughout the whole expanse of history it requires nothing in return but a fresh, green, and vitalizing response to its encouragement.

For Hildegard, green is not a mere colour but a basic attitude and purposive intent. It is the permanent inflowing and outflowing of *viriditas*, the symbol of sound existence. Ultimately, physical health is a lasting and continuously effective outpouring of this greening power from the inexhaustible fountain of life's living light. This conviction allows Hildegard to praise the *viriditas nobilissima* (most noble greenness) that is rooted in the sun, shining like the dawn, radiating its brightness, in an eternal cycle whose ultimacy and complexity the human mind can never fully grasp (S 108). It is greenness shining in the motion of the cosmos and in the wheel of history; it is the vitalizing ground of all life laid down and tilled by the creative hand of God (*viriditas digiti Dei*). God planted the wonderfully illuminated and illuminative creation in evergreen freshness. It is the fragrant breath of greenness that leads our spirit too into the broad expanses of the world, exhaling wisdom to be inhaled by our hearts together with the very joy of being alive (S 137).

Finest green of all greens showing,
From the sun's strength ever growing,

Enclosed in everlasting love,
Fed from a boundless source above,

Embraced by mysteries divine
That all our earthly thoughts outshine.

Like each new dawn, renewed delight,
To all the world a gift of light,

Like the sun's flames ever glowing,
Noblest, greenest green now flowing.

(S 109)

Healing and life

Human beings were originally created to be healthy and whole. Health and wholeness are the basic characteristics of the human constitution. "For God has not only restored human beings, who began well but then fell into misery, but summoned them to an even higher vocation and more blessed state by giving them the capacities to achieve a holy life" (LVM I, 47). People cooperate with God by playing their part in the divine work of creation (*operarius divinitatis*). This means that they are responsible for cultivating the world (*opus cum creatura*). Both the cosmic cycle and the course of history provide human activity with the fresh life-giving force (*viriditas*) that produces flower and fruit, or leads to useful development and change. In her manual on the art of healing ("Causae et curae"), Hildegard provides an appropriate (if initially delphic) summary formula for this process: "The reality of the Word becomes fruitful in greenness" (CaCu 22, 15: *opus verbi viriditas*).

When Adam and Eve were driven out of Paradise and into the world, they found that night had already fallen upon the earth. "But they also found that it was already equipped with everything that suited their human nature, and with all the vital necessities (*necessaria*), both for themselves and for all other forms of life, so they appropriated all this potential and all these facilities for their own use" (PL 223 A). They used the apparently wholly natural circumstances of existence in the world to satisfy their existential needs. They soon discovered, however, that everything had to be carefully and expertly cultivated: breathing and eating and drinking as much as labour and celebration, waking and sleeping and all our activities, whether in sorrow or in joy. But we have been endowed with all these physical needs so that we can find out what is good for us and then arrange things and adjust ourselves accordingly (LVM IV, 12: *unde homo praevideat, quid sibi prosit*).

After all, subjecting ourselves to a fixed set of rules in our everyday life is part and parcel of a sensible lifestyle. It is an essential feature of the order of existence which people either have to devise for themselves (*sive per ipsum*) or to receive and accept from someone else (*sive per alium*). It is quite natural for humankind (LDO IV, 73: *ei naturale est*) to conduct their lives in this way, for all nature has an underlying impulse to move from a natural toward a cultivated state.

This vital order of life is based on the wise understanding, the profound physiological insight, as it were, that the same basic needs (*res naturales*) can either sustain or destroy the inner conditions of life (*res non naturales*).

For Hildegard, discretion (*discretio*), which includes the capacity of discrimination, is the mother of all the virtues (*mater virtutum*) and the decisive criterion for allocating all the necessities of life within the range of possibilities open to us. *Discretio* is the very root (*radix prima*) of all activity, and the "firmament" of life on earth. "The earthly dispensation, which means active life, practises discretion, whereas the heavenly dispensation, or contemplative life, is subject to it." Knowing the mean, behaving with due measure, exerts a healing function and dresses all irregularity to decent order (*discretio temperat omnia*).

The foregoing may be summarized by saying that for Hildegard the fundamental principle of the healing art is the natural life-force (*viriditas*). It is the source of our enjoyment of existence pure and simple, and of our pleasure in shaping it meaningfully (*constitutio*). Inevitably, we all have to experience the inadequacies, disappointments, and even wretchedness of life (*destitutio*). In one way or another, we all come to regret the loss of the world in all its pristine beauty. But that is all the more reason to fight passionately for its

58. Discretio
The figure of "Discretion" is seated on a stone at the bottom end of the threefold wall. She moves a crucifix to and fro with her shoulder to indicate the tension between justice and mercy. She uses her fan to ward off all attempts to dissuade her. A beam of light reaches her body and illumines her face.

Liber Scivias, copy of the former Rupertsberg Codex, c. 1180; (detail from Fig. 8) St Hildegard's Abbey, Eibingen

*61. **Christus medicus: Christ healing a Hunchback*** from the Prayer Book ascribed to Hildegard of Bingen,

Middle Rhine provenance, *c.* 1190; Cod. Lat. 935, fol. 26v Munich, Bavarian State Library

119

Images of mercy

For Hildegard, mercy is the guiding principle of all medical practice. It is embodied in *Christus Medicus*. He is the great Physician (*magnus medicus*) who cares for sick people seeking treatment and longing to be made whole and healthy once more (Sc I, 3). "The good physician (*bonus medicus*) does not delay but applies the balm of compassion and consolation to human wounds with the utmost speed" (Bw 154).

It is not by accident that this mercy wears the green garment of the fresh life-force, the *viriditas* that Hildegard praises as the "King's most beautiful companion." The means by which mercy is proffered are comfort and patience; it takes the form of discretion; it offers the possibilities of repentance and conversion; and its ultimate goal is salvation. Hildegard calls it the worst of all evils (*pessimum malum malorum*) when things get so bad that "no one any longer takes interest in his or her neighbour's health and cannot be bothered to show compassion to anyone" (LVM I, 83).

It was Mary in particular, the "exemplary Mother of the holy art of healing," who poured her medicinal oil into the wounds of death.

Mary is the "mediatrix of life," the "joy of total radiance," the "fragrance of all delights." She is the means by which we gain access to mercy as the supreme medicine for our wounds and woes (*magna medicina*) and as "the gentlest of healing herbs in air and dew and all-revivifying freshness" (LVM I, 17).

Mercy is the primary means by which the human heart becomes a pure stream. "For the more people pay attention to themselves and to their own health and in this way get control of themselves and empower their own lives, the more prepared and able they are to show compassionate love to their fellow-humans when they need help." After all, God himself shows mercy to human beings, assumes the burdens of our miseries, pours the "wine of forgiveness" into our wounds and anoints us with the "oil of mercy" (LDO V, 46). Accordingly, when they are afflicted the faithful look for doctors and consult them before they sicken mortally and die. Doctors prescribe a "bitter herbal remedy" but also offer the wine of forgiveness and the oil of mercy (Sc I, 4).

We cannot fail to notice the major part played by sighing and weeping, sobbing and contrition in Hildegard's writings and the very physical ways in which all these movements "of the soul" are expressed. This is because the whole human being is moved to remorse and contrition, becomes agitated, learns to open up, achieves insight and self-knowledge, and reaches the point of conversion and renewal. Penitence makes its contribution to this process, just as (according to Hildegard) a woman contributes her knowledge and ability to a man's efforts in life.

The sighing of the human heart expresses its inner turmoil and elevation, those salutary convulsions that are necessary before it is wholly renewed. "The quickest way to peace is a change of heart," says Hildegard, and adds: "The heart is the source of health or destruction. In fact, the human heart is the centre of the world." On another occasion, when writing to Pope Anastasius IV, she says: "It is the heart that heals and saves when the dawn comes up with all the splendour of the first sunrise" (Bw 40).

The virtue of the "knowledge of God" is a merciful gift. It seems as fearsome and terrible (*terribilis in terrore*) as it is kind-hearted and gentle (*lenis in bonitate*). It appears everywhere and in everything (*apud omnia et in omnibus*), and "it is so mysteriously beautiful that none of us can really know the immense ramifications of the love with which it sustains us and, by stretching mercy to infinity, protects us" (Sc III, 4).

Penitence as the "illumination of the soul" is depicted as a prime remedy (*quasi medicina*) and as a vitally refreshing and healing power for the human heart (*viriditas poenitentiae*). People experience an inward shock and an upheaval, but as a result the healing power of repentance leads them out of misery and restores them to life. Tears, then, revivify and liberate us; they make hard hearts tender and summon the Holy Spirit to our aid. They coax *viriditas* out again so that it wells up in us as that ever-renewed and ever-green, creative, refreshing, and rejuvenating life-force by which we advance along the sure path to everlasting light.

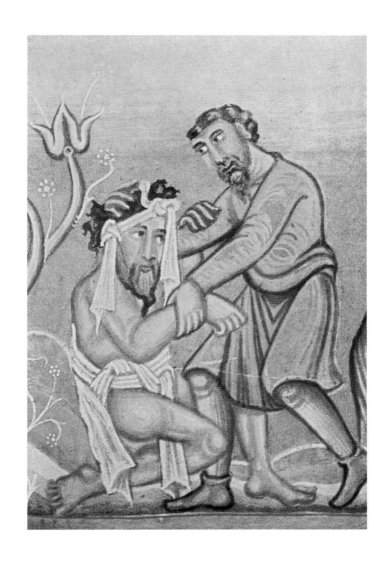

62. **The Good Samaritan**
Gospels of Heinrich III.
Echternach, 1045/46;
Cod. Lat. Vetrinas 17,
Escorial, Patrimonio
Nacional

Mercy's message for Hardness of Heart:

The plants exchange the fragrance of their flowers, and precious stones offer one another their brilliant gleam. Every living thing longs for some other's loving embrace. All nature serves humanity and supplies its treasures in love and joy. But all you provide, you obdurate creature, is a harsh gaze and bleak smoke in the darkness.

But I am the infinitely sweet herb of mercy. I am to be found in the air, in the dew, and in all the fresh greenness of life. My heart is overflowing with readiness to help all those in need. I was already there when 'Let there be...!' was uttered, and the world that now serves humankind emerged. You, Hardness of Heart, have no such loving core of being, whereas I, Mercy, observe all life's needs with my kindly eye, and feel close to everything that is. I help the weak and fragile, and guide them towards health and wholeness. I am a soothing balm for every sorrow, and my consoling words restore people in body and in soul.

(LVM I, 17)

*63. **Lily.*** Liber floridus,
Ms. 92, fol. 230
Geneva, University Library

5. True salvation

64. Christ's Sacrifice and the Church
The Church receives its life from the wound in the side of the crucified Saviour. At the altar the Church requests the "precious wedding-present" of the Lord's Body and Blood.

Liber Scivias, copy of the former Rupertsberg Codex, *c.* 1180; St Hildegard's Abbey, Eibingen.

Creation and redemption

Under the headings of the key-terms *homo constitutus* and *genitura mystica* (humanity as originally planned in the mystery of its origin) Hildegard provides a comprehensive physiology of humanity in the dispensation of Adam. She depicts people as they originated, in their *constitutio prima*, or original constitution, as they were first designed to be. These humans were light through and through, and radiated light from the *lumen corporis*, the luminance of their bodies. The whole world was available to them in their *natura gloriosa*, or radiant nature. This "nature" is not the *physis* proposed by the natural philosophy of classical antiquity. Something new has been added to it that exceeds the capacity of all images, concepts, and terminology: Christ, the Son of the cosmos, who assumed human nature in order to transform and redeem created beings.

Salvation history also sheds light on the present nature of human existence, the sickness of people in the state of *natura deficiens* (nature unnatural), and in the distress brought about by *destitutio*, *deformatio*, and *degeneratio* (inadequacy, distortion, and depravation). Essentially, humanity (*homo destitutus*) has departed from its original state. It has become fragile and sick. People now lead lives of care and anxiety. They are corrupt and draw ever closer to the void, for they fail in their intended work and are untrue to the Word. They lose their original freshness, their *viriditas*, growing so weak and unstable that they constantly leave the true lines of authentic existence, and move from health into sickness.

Human beings' original *constitutio*, therefore, gave way to *destitutio*, to malformation and decadence, to degradation, dissension, and discordance. It now calls for a general and particular *restitutio*, or restoration to consonance and harmony; it requires the healing and redemption of the whole person. We need

integritas, or what is known in Arabic as *salam*. This is not merely peace and quietude but wholeness, healing, total well-being: the reintegration of human nature, its restitution and rehabilitation: in short, its salvation. All human life, indeed, may be seen as a dialogue about redemption.

The world as it actually develops forces us to inquire ever more deeply and so to speak to "penetrate" (*penetrare*), to delve into and interpret it anew, and to probe and discover the burgeoning, unfolding manifestations of the universe (*plenitudo profectus in crescendo*). Without these natural phenomena, and without their evolution, we would remain blind, inert, and childish, knowing nothing about ourselves or about God. Our roots in nature (*plantatio in prima radice*) prompt us ever onward until we become fellow-citizens (*socii*) in the heavenly homeland.

In this respect, the all-originating hand of God is always at work and the Body of Christ is ever-present. The design of God's handiwork (*factura digiti Dei*) is evident as well as the vital force of his hand (*viriditas digiti Dei*) by which he has planted all that is designed and summoned to emerge in glory and resplendence.

Human nature is essentially directed to cooperation in the completion and fulfilment of creation. Human beings become so to speak participants and sharers in divine revelation, in all these ways to salvation. Without this very practical commission to act in and on the world, an *opus cum creatura* until the end of the world, the universe would remain chaotic, nothing but *materia turbulenta* (chaotic matter), and the world would still be unseeing and shapeless.

It is only in this formative and educative process that human beings are able to come to be themselves and to restore the beautiful cosmos to due order. By carrying out their own *opus* (work) in the course of their *vita humana* (authentic human life), people play their various parts in the great symphony of vital joy and happiness (*symphonia vitae laetae*).

Hildegard praises all the expressions of human virtue (*virtutes*) that become evident on this path to redemption, particularly since they emanate from God, the "chief source of all true joy" (Sc III, 9). The virtues work in concert to help people to maturity (*ad profectum hominis*). Everything serves the process of maturation in the Holy Spirit, whom Hildegard lauds in one of her hymns as "the innermost heart and vital force of all nature" (*vita vitae creaturae*), and as the healing "fire of love" constantly bent on universal sanctification (*divina vis salvare vult*), and directed to the one goal of health and salvation.

The spiritual principles supporting Hildegard's wholly optimistic view of the world are clear, consistent and unmistakable:

God appears as the one Godhead in three-fold form. In his Son (*verbum*) God creates his work (*opus*), the world, and humanity. But the whole world exists only by virtue of the vital power (*viriditas*) of the Holy Spirit.

The Word is intended to become flesh in this created world, and in fact did so and dwelled among us. This design was part of the Father's will from the very beginning. God wanted to reveal himself to the whole world in human form.

God is the Shepherd of existence and the summons from the commencement of all that is, by whom all creation came into existence. He not only made us but liberates us from all suffering and misery and frees us from the sickness which we all seem condemned to fall into.

The whole world is called to redemption in the Word (*logos*). At the end of the ages, the whole world will be transfigured and enabled to enter a new heaven and a new earth. Genesis and Apocalypse will discover their true meaning and destiny in the cosmic Christ, the world's Saviour.

Human beings make their way through the world in conformity with the cycle of nature, in accordance with the dispositions of time, and by following the saving path of their history. At the beginning of time God allowed his creations to progress like a radiant sun. He not only led them into the light but made sure that they continued to develop to the due point of their fulfillment. Divine life assures us of a "profusion of fruitfulness for the further development of all creation."

Whatever humans have decided on in their innermost being they enact externally, in the world, in *opus cum creatura* (together with creation). "A path leads from the human heart to the elements of the cosmos." This light in the "eye of the heart" is the source of vitality for everything dry and withered. Wheat and corn grow by virtue of the mysterious green force that courses and pours through the germinating powers of the cosmos and in the healing powers of history. "When human beings have a sure foot on the pathway of the heart (*iter cordis*), they are helping to construct the roadway by which all things will come home to God."

As physical and sexual creatures enmeshed in their physicality and sexuality, acted on and acting on the world, human beings are intended to cooperate with all the elements, always so to speak courting nature and constantly redrafting and rediscovering the world. In themselves, human beings are images of creation and of redemption. God gave them the gift of a life to be lived in joy and freedom of mind and spirit. They are designed to lead truly rational and spiritual lives.

In their special location, suspended as it were between creation and redemption, human beings are granted the possibility of a free choice and consequently are given full responsibility for what they choose. "Therefore people should not allow any other aspect of creation in the world to determine what they do. Instead they should plan and carry it out on the basis of their own nature (*per semetipsum*), just as God uses no other material but himself for his creation" (LVM VI, 59). In the turning wheel or sphere of our conscience (*rota scientiae*) we are very well aware of the right direction to take in what we do (LVM III, 27). "And so humans do not have some special star that decides their fate in life, as foolish people believe." Accordingly, God does not want people to consult stars, fire, birds, and the like about what the future may hold (Sc I, 3).

In conscientious love (*in scientia caritatis*), God wants to guide his image and likeness—though in total freedom—to enjoy "the full benefits of wholeness" (*ad plentitudinem*

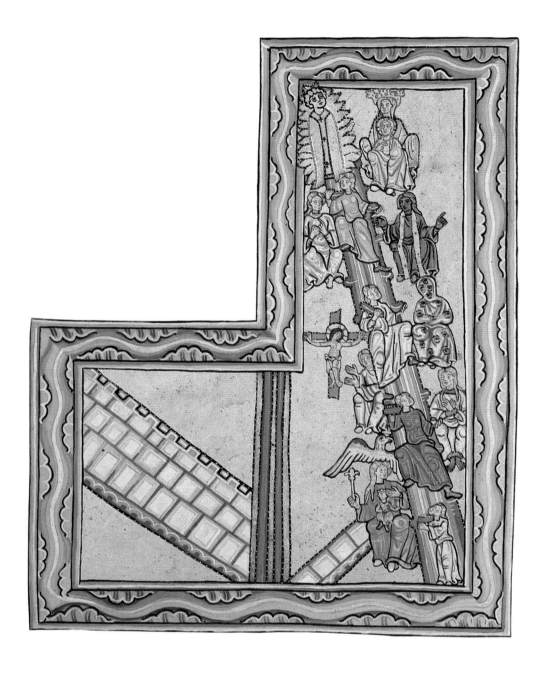

65. *The Divine Virtues carrying Stones for a Building*

The Virtues help people to complete God's saving work.

Liber Scivias, copy of the former Rupertsberg Codex. St Hildegard's Abbey, Eibingen

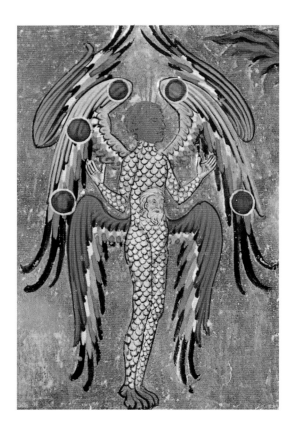

66. Omnipotence
The figure of Omnipotence with a fiery-red face and scaly body below the "City of God." The head of an old man on the front of the figure represents the plan of salvation in God the *Father. The five mirrors stand for the various epochs of salvation history.* Liber Divinorum Operum, *c. 1240; Ms. 1942 (detail), Lucca, Biblioteca Statale*

67. The Redeemer
Fallen humanity is still struggling in a darkness illuminated by patriarchs and prophets. A bright Figure preparing to redeem fallen humankind emerges *from the background of God's creation.* Liber Scivias, *copy of the former Rupertsberg Codex, c. 1180; St Hildegard's Abbey, Eibingen*

integritatis) (LDO I, 11). Therefore humans are not helplessly exposed to some kind of anarchic freedom. God himself will take them under his wings like a chicken with her brood. "For God did not want to enjoy his glory for himself alone. He wanted to communicate it to his creatures, so that they could enjoy it together with him" (LVM I, 136).

But this means that human beings have to decide for themselves and to take responsibility for all their dealings with the world. They find themselves in the middle of a "dispute conducted by the virtues (*ordo virtutum*)" and constantly engaged in a struggle with the vices and with the difficulties and risks that are factors of our everyday life.

Hildegard dramatizes the contest between the virtues and vices as in a minor morality play. One telling example is the particularly harsh role enacted by the character she calls "Hardness of Heart." This imaginary form materializes like a dense cloud of smoke and tries its best to look human, with signal lack of success. It moves neither forward nor backward but remains motionless in the dark from which its black eyes stare at the visionary. It says: "I'm totally unproductive. I've achieved nothing in the world and I've brought no one into existence. Why should I care about anything or worry about anybody? As far as I'm concerned, things should stay just as they are. I only interfere when someone could be of use to me. God made everything, so he can look after it all and care for his own odds and ends... All I'm concerned about is my own existence. You should all do the same and just look after Number One!" (LVM I, 16).

Hardness of Heart, moral sclerocardia, appears here as a vice centred on the waste and misuse of time. When human beings grow tired of their ineffably banal activity and pointless effort their loathing for life "turns to hardness of heart." Once their hearts have hardened people can no longer recognize God's image in their neighbours. Hardness of heart means that it is like a lump of lead falling to the bottom of a pool and just lying there motionless. "It is the worst of all such afflictions because it has no time for anyone and shows no one mercy. It is sheer numbness. It treats humanity as something contemptible. It means that people cannot really enjoy being with others, and it certainly stops them from helping others. It is just total indiffer-

ence, obduracy, and absence of any feeling" (LVM I, 83).

Another particularly injurious attitude alongside hardness of heart is unabashed deceit. Hildegard calls it "the vice of inhumanity." If someone sins out of a desire for physical pleasure, that is at least understandable and still thoroughly human, "but people given to mendacity have overstepped the bounds of humanity." They have simply forgotten and lost the joy of life (LVM II, 83).

The virtues, however, can promptly muster a more than competent force in the struggle again the numerically powerful company of vices—all thirty-five of them. In addition to mercy (*misericordia*), patience (*patientia*) is particularly effective in "pouring out a healing balm." As Patience itself says: "I am the tender breath of all that is green and fresh. I make it possible for the flowers and fruits of the virtues to emerge and build a strong fortress for them in the human heart" (LVM I, 23).

Hildegard's accounts of mercy as a salve for every affliction, as comfort in all necessity, and as a ready help in trouble show us that it is one of the fundamental principles of her understanding of the world and its ways. She constantly reminds us to: "Show that you care about people whenever you can!" "Look after your fellow-humans as long as you still have eyes to see them!" "Be a beacon to your neighbours and treat them with a mother's tender care!"

In this context, too, Hildegard refers to love between male and female. She sees it as essentially paralleling the love between the Creator and his creation, as we find it expressed in the Song of Solomon:

"But Solomon, wise not only in mind and spirit but in feeling and sensitivity, speaks like a lover and as if addressing his beloved. I, however, am Wisdom itself (*sapientia*) and this is what I mean by what I inspired Solomon to say: 'Then I rose up and took off my robe in order to drench it in thousands upon thousands of drops of precious dew.' God (as it were) says this to show that he intends this costly gift for humans and relies on their commitment. 'Let us enter into true dialogue with one another' (he says).

"Ordaining all things as I made my way through the heavens, I, Wisdom, inspired by the Creator's love for his creatures, and by their love for their Creator, also spoke to

Solomon and inspired him to say the following in his own words: The Creator has adorned his creation, the creature of his own making, with the gift of his great love. Accordingly all obedience on the part of human creatures is no more than their expression of their profound desire to be embraced by the Creator. And, in fact, the whole world was kissed by its Creator when God endowed it with everything that it could possibly need" (LVM V, 39).

But humans are and remain the very essence of creation. God kisses humanity, his very own work (*officiale opus*) with his loving lips. Out of sheer love he gave people the world for them to enjoy and work with (*officium omnis creaturae*). As if with one voice, the whole creation will rejoice over this (*in symphonia sonet*). All the harps of heaven will be heard and will contribute to its great orchestral harmony (*ad caelestem harmoniam*). The angels will add their hymns of praise to this general rejoicing (*in laudibus*). Everything will resound in total resplendent concord. "We must remember, too, that through their capacity for praise (*laus*), or celebration, human beings also enjoy an angelic nature, though in their active capacity, in their sanctifying work (*opus*), they are human. Considered in all their aspects, however, they are the complete work of God (*plenum opus Dei*), since God expresses and fulfils his wonders in humans both in the form of celebration and in that of activity" (LVM V, 96).

God made humans together with all the rest of creation, "to make sure that they would not lead a solitary life on this earth but be images and likenesses of God himself in this respect too. After all, God is not alone in heaven, for he is glorified by all the melodies sung by all the heavenly choirs."

God will restore the appearance of beauty to humans, for he desires perfection and wholeness. Then people will be clothed in glory. They will pour forth songs constantly surpassing one another in novelty, singing in unison with the choir of angels—those angels who "watch the eternal Heart beating at the very source of creation" and see, as if in the countenance of God, "the breath that issues from the innermost pulsation of the Father's Heart" (S 67).

The saints in heaven will be hills spread with flowers in a landscape of pure delight: flowers of the meadows and of the fields, tender green shoots, perfect fruit and precious living vessels filled to overflowing with natural fragrance among which the Holy Spirit will sing for ever.

68. **An Angelic Choir**
Above the "City of God,"
which stands for the still
unfinished work of
salvation, the visionary

sees a group of musicians
with various instruments
in a cloud—an anticipa-
tion of the angelic choirs of
Paradise.

Detail, Liber Divinorum
Operum,
c. 1240; Ms 1942,
Lucca, Biblioteca Statale

131

Paths to salvation

Hildegard explains the destiny of fallen humankind and the route it must take to healing and salvation in terms taken from the biblical parable of the unjust steward (Luke 16:1-8). The steward who was formerly so gifted and richly endowed is dispossessed and deprived of his inheritance; he becomes biologically deficient. To justify himself he makes an agreement with the world so that he can escape from his alienated existence and find a new position as a steward. Wiser than the children of light, the angels whose hearts are hardened and set in an evil disposition, human beings acquire friends by honest cultivation. The restoration of the cosmos to health and wholeness is seen not only as a matter of quite practical action in, with, and on nature, in a setting of cosmic cooperation as it were; it is compared to the bride being taken to the wedding, to the reunion of Creator and creation in a transfigured world.

Hildegard also explains the essential association of creation and redemption in terms of two key figures of whom she is especially fond: Eve, the original material (*prima materia*) of the human race, the "mother of all living creatures," and Mary, the *aurea materia*, or Mother of salvation and healing (*mater medicinae*). As Mother of salvation (*salvatrix*) she gathers up the members of the Son's body and restores them to heavenly harmony (*ad caelestem harmoniam*).

In Mary that most beautiful flower that had been dry and withered since the time of Eve recovers its freshness and offers its sweet fragrance to all humanity. Now everything is restored to its full vitality: "The heavens give the grass their dew and the whole earth rejoices. Its womb is filled with wheat once again. The birds are rebuilding their nests. Now humans have food once more and there is great rejoicing at their banquet." Mary, "joy of all joys," has presented us with all this (S 151).

Because of her great humility Mary was chosen to become the King's secret bridal chamber (*clausus cubiculus regis*). God himself decided to dwell in her modest womb. But at the time when God promised Abraham a race of descendants "as plenteous as the stars in heaven," he already foresaw the race that would eventually form the "full company of heavenly community" (LDO I, 17).

When Mary the Star of the Sea shone out, all the elements reacquired the "joy of life." "The heavens were fiery red and the whole world sang the praises of Mary!" The Star of the Sea will shine out over the fulfilled creation and the whole universe will be renewed for ever as a new creation, an authentic "cosmos," a system truly representing and containing all and everything.

In spite of all the honour and respect she has for Mary, as is particularly evident in her *Symphonia*, Hildegard never mentions any of the well-known Mariological tropes, such as the *Mater dolorosa* (Mother of Sorrows), the Immaculate Conception, the Assumption, May devotions to Mary, and so on. Mary's role is that of a "second Eve." It is centred entirely on the Incarnation. For Hildegard, Mary is the means by which heaven is all the more beautifully arrayed, as beautifully as the earth was once sadly led astray by Eve (S 53).

Hildegard's treatment of these central human figures also reminds us that God's blessings are dependent, very dependent indeed, on women. It is from woman that God's benefits spread over the whole earth. For God became a human being in a young woman, in a woman who was the unique focus of love and happiness (S 47). The amount of happiness and truly blessed existence that emerges from this woman is incalculable. Woman is the source of the sweet fragrance of the virtues and all their powers, which pour and stream from her (S 53). Mary is the most beautiful, the most delightful, of all women. She pleased God so much that he filled her with the warmth of his love so that his Son could feed at her breast. Then her body rejoiced and the sound of all the heavens playing in concert resounded from her heart.

Hildegard repeatedly praises Mary lyrically as "bright flower," "fair flower," "blossoming in the light of dawn," and so forth. Her body sprang with the sensation of joy like grass on which the dew has fallen.

Hildegard celebrates woman as the "Sister of Wisdom." Wisdom herself is represented as a woman and as the "eye of God," before whose countenance she stands as his "beloved companion."

Those who see God and those who proclaim him are heaven. Heaven was manifest when the Son of God appeared in human form. And those angels are heaven who shine out like fire flaming from God's radiant light, and through whom God vanquished all his enemies. But when God made heaven and earth he placed human beings at the centre of the universe and put everything at their disposal. And their work of mediation is related to that of the Mediator, God the Son, and the centre of their world to the centre of God's heart, where he dwells. Just as a decision issues from the human heart, so the Son emerged from God the Father. For the heart knows its reason and it dwells in the heart. The heart and the heart's decision are one, and there can be no distinction between them.

(LDO IX, 9)

*69. **Mary***
Detail, Liber Scivias,
copy of the former
Rupertsberg Codex,
c. 1180;
St Hildegard's Abbey,
Eibingen

70. One of the Forms of the Church
The figure of a strong and powerful woman, representing the mystical body of the Church, emerges from silver mountain- peaks. A calyx opening in every direction grows from her chest, and at its centre stands the minute red-clad figure of Mary, also described by Hildegard as the "Sister of Wisdom."

Liber Scivias, copy of the former Rupertsberg Codex, c. 1180; St Hildegard's Abbey, Eibingen

The office of the Church

In another vision in Book 2 of *Scivias* (Know the Ways), Hildegard describes her encounter with the figure of *Ecclesia* (the Church), and tells us how the initial construction-works for the everlasting dwelling-places of a wholesome world are made ready even on this earth.

"After this I saw the vision of a tall woman. She was as imposing as a great city and had a wonderful and beautifully decorated crown on her head. A lustrous shower of extraordinary brilliance descended from her arms almost like sleeves shimmering and shining from heaven to earth. Her womb was like a giant net with many apertures through which a great throng of people passed. I could not see any clothing on this woman, but she was entirely suffused with a brilliant light and totally enclosed in gleaming splendour. Daybreak glowed and glistened on her breast, and from everywhere about her I heard that sparkling dawn singing a glorious medley of tunes of every kind.

"This figure radiated such splendour that it seemed to flow about her like a garment. As I looked, she began to speak: 'I must conceive and give birth!' Immediately a band of angels hastened toward her. They prepared steps and seats in her for all the people who would bring the figure to perfection. Then I saw a great number of little children close to the ground swimming through the air like fishes in water. They made their way through the openings in the figure and entered her womb. She drew her breath in sharply and pulled them up to her head, whereupon they flew out of her mouth. So she remained quite unharmed by them" (Sc II, 3).

The figure Hildegard is describing is Mother Church, whose womb is like the "earth gestating" and longing to bear fruit. The Church is the "earth of the living fruit of good works," which it brings forth in the "vitality of faith" (LDO V, 33). It has become like the "living earth." Just as a huge city receives vast crowds of people of many nations, and just as a broad net takes up a great quantity of fishes, so Mother Church accepts the company of the faithful and remains the "country of the living." In baptism, and only once, she gives every earthly life a gift of great price, which here on earth can already gleam and shimmer as a reflection of the ultimate splendour of eternal life.

All this allows the Church to be termed "the virgin Mother of all Christians." Through the power of the Holy Spirit she receives and bears children and presents them to God, so that they may be known henceforth as the "children of God." She does this out of an inexhaustible motherly love that she extends to all people, ready to receive, hold, support, and heal them. "Just as balsam flows from a tree, and just as healing medicines (*fortissimae medicinae*) are poured from an onyx jar, and just as a garnet sends out rays of purest light, so the Son of God was born from the Virgin's womb." Just as the Holy Spirit overshadowed Mary, the blessed Mother of God's Son, so that she could conceive and bear without pain, so the Holy Spirit now sheds light on and through the Church, "the happy Mother of all the faithful" (Sc II, 3).

The Church is not like any natural institution or, indeed, any other community. It represents the incursion of divine life into the order of human society. The most valuable and authentic aspects of the Church are not the ecclesiastical structures, which have developed in history and have been shaped by doctrine, but its true efficacy and ultimate reality, which have a purely metaphysical significance.

Of course the Church also has a specific history and a certain destiny which is also definable by knowledge of that history. Hildegard tells us how she came to realize this when her vision took a highly dramatic turn. She shows us the remarkable figure of another woman, seen now in the half-light of earlier times. As this strange yet majestic figure approaches, we see that the lower part of its body appears to be clad in black, whereas its feet are blood-red and a brilliant white cloud flows round them. Black, red, and white; the contrast could not be starker.

This is the Synagogue, which seems to be purblind and somehow inactive, for it stands near the altar but does not touch it. Yet it is granted the Redeemer's blood which it draws up through its feet. The white cloud dispenses the essential gift of life. In Hildegard's scheme of things the Synagogue, with Abraham at its origin and Moses in its breast, is presented as the first-fruits of faith, a forerunner of the Church. The end of the Synagogue is the dawn of the Church.

For Hildegard the Synagogue is not to be condemned or despised in any way. Instead it is to be praised and respected as a forerunner and to be given its correct place in the history of salvation. The Synagogue also sees God's mysteries in shadowy form without disclosing them fully (Sc I, 5). "The old Law was only the sound of the approaching Word, the shadow as it were of Christ, the resounding Word himself" (LVM I, 40).

Hildegard depicts the Synagogue respect-fully and tenderly (this is especially notewor-thy if we consider many of the crude and erroneous things that were said about it even in her time), but she realizes that "the God of Abraham, Isaac, and Jacob" appears only as the God of his people: a God who openly denies himself to other nations. But that would imply a Spirit that is not available to all, which is unacceptable. Yet the Synagogue, together with Moses and the Prophets, is the chosen bearer of a great Promise. Therefore Hildegard's title for it, and for the figure that represents it, is impressive: the Synagogue is the "Mother of the Incarnation (*mater incarnationis*)." "Just as the dawn disappears and gives way to full sunlight, so the Old Testament is in the background of the Gospel's truth. The Synagogue was the precursor of the Church in the light of truth" (Sc I, 5).

Ecclesia, the Church, appeared in its full stature when it emerged from the open wound in Jesus' side. Now it is a living figure, and shows us the open chalice in which it receives the blood flowing from the side of Christ, for the humanity of Christ is the basis upon which the Church is built (*Humanitas Christi est principium omnis aedificationis sanctae ecclesiae*). A new world has appeared, the world of grace manifest in the "birth of righteous-ness." The origin of the Church has been in the Father's heart since the beginning; and in the wound in the Son's side, in Christ's sacrifice, and in the Holy Spirit's fiery breath of life.

In this Spirit, Hildegard tell us, the King of heaven appointed the "holders of the various offices of divine service," so that they might "act prudently, wisely, and faithfully" to "oversee the care of souls and to support people physically (*ad curam animarum et ad sustentationem corporum*)" (Sc II, 6). They are the guides chosen to accompany the people of God on their pilgrim way, which reaches ever onward.

Hildegard depicts the Church as a very beautiful woman in yet another context. "She is exceptionally attractive and of a beauty beyond human comprehension." The figure of the Church towers high above the earth, so high that it reaches into the heavens above. Its face is extraordinarily radiant. It is dressed in pure silk and is adorned with precious stones. "But her face is covered in dust and her robe is torn on the right side," and her shoes are filthy.

This imperfect figure is also the Church, which constantly changes like the moon (*in circuitione motionis*). "Many of her children grow in virtue, whereas others slacken and change course, because their behaviour is inconsistent or they are rent by contradiction." As a result, the Church follows something approaching a lunar orbit (Sc II, 5). Yet it carries all the treasures of wisdom and know-ledge in its womb; it develops as the "city where all branches of knowledge are to be found (*urbs scientarum*);" and it offers Chris-tians the means by which they can reach their intended maturity.

The Church offers salvation not only to individual humans but to all creation. It is the all-embracing sacrament of redemption. "Christ came to disclose the innermost nature of the law, for he changed the water of the law into the wine of the Gospel, and thus allowed the strong currents of the virtues to flow freely and generously" (Sc III, 11). "When God made humans, he inscribed the whole creation (*omnis creatura*) in them, just as you might

*71. **The Synagogue***
Liber Scivias, copy of the former Rupertsberg Codex, *c.* 1180; St Hildegard's Abbey, Eibingen

*72. **Blood flowing from the Side of Christ***
Detail, Liber Scivias, copy of the former Rupertsberg Codex, *c.* 1180; St Hildegard's Abbey, Eibingen

73. **The Fountain of Life**
*Three female figures stand
as if rooted in, or on the
stone rim of, the Fountain*
*of Life above the City of
God, and look up to
contemplate his saints in a
heavenly cloud.*
Liber Divinorum
Operum, *c.* 1240; Ms
1942 (detail)
Lucca, Biblioteca Statale.

write the times and statistics of an entire year on a single scrap of parchment. That is why God called humanity 'the whole creation'" (Bw 176).

It was not a Spirit encompassing the universe that actually illuminated and enlightened it, but a woman's quietly gestating womb. Humanity is God's first great love, and God wants to commemorate his betrothal in love. The virgin Church—the Son's bride—has become the mother of salvation history, bearing fruit in the form of her faithful children. "Like the fragrance of sweet-smelling plants, the community of the Church emerges from the depths of love in the mystery of the Father's heart." God has never ceased to rejoice at being among the children of humankind.

God's Golden City

Human beings can sanctify their short lives on earth by helping to build the "Golden City of God" (*civitas aurea*), a project that will reach its final phase in the new creation of a transfigured world. This will come about when Mother Church leads home the children whom she has cherished, and ushers them into the everlasting concordance of heavenly harmony (*superna symphonia*). The City is a many-facetted image in Hildegard's works, with echoes from scripture, the Fathers, and other sacred writers. It stands for the history of salvation. It is also a symbol of eternal life in the heavenly Jerusalem. God's Son entered the world and began the process of its sanctification, of making it as naturally holy as it was intended to be. The dramatic advance of salvation history will continue until the community of God's children inhabits the longed-for Golden City of God definitively, as the Communion of Saints.

The Golden City represents the Church itself. Its cornerstone is the Incarnation of the Son of God (LDO V, 18). The members of Christ's Body dwell in the Golden City as the perfect community of beauty fulfilled. The Bride in all her beauty is an imposing woman, as mighty as a city (Sc III,11: *pulcherrima sponsa, scilicet Ecclesia*). "The building of living souls reaches completion" by using live stones until "the beauty of its wonders has matured in the purity of faith" (Sc II, 3).

Then the Church will appear most beautifully arrayed in gold and precious metalwork. Its eyes will be like sapphires, its nose like a mountain of myrrh, and its mouth like the gush and sparkle of many streams. "Humans are wonderfully like the surging and billowing of the sea when they, otherwise so inconstant in their mere fickle flowing hither and thither, are aroused by the fire of the Holy Spirit and rise up from an earthly to a heavenly plane" (LDO IX, 8).

Now three resplendent figures, Love, Humility, and Peace, appear above the mighty City, standing in the "Fountain of Life," or on its rim. The first of the figures begins to speak: "I am Love, and I am the glory of the living God. Wisdom is my partner in all I do; Humility, who is rooted in the living Fountain, is my helper; and Peace is her companion. The living light of the blessed angels shines out by drawing on the glory of my being. This glory is luminous in the blessed angels. It must shine out like that because there can be no light without luminance. I designed human beings so that they might know their roots in me and be, as it were, my reflections, just as each and every thing is reflected in water. Just so, I Love am a living stream, and everything in creation dwells in me as if reflected in a stream."

Just as all creation is reflected in love, so God became human in humility, "in order to lift up and restore to blessedness the withered leaves that had fallen," and thus to redeem all things and reinstate the universal reign of peace. "Therefore rivers of living water are to be poured out over the whole world, to ensure that people, like fishes caught in a net, can be restored to wholeness" (LDO VII, 2).

Just as David carried the head of the vanquished Philistine Goliath to Jerusalem, "my Son in the humility of his body bore this head into the holy Church and into the 'vision of peace'" (Sc III, 1), in that city of peace which, accordingly, is also called "Jerusalem."

Consequently the Church now stands before us all as a supremely beautiful construction, gleaming in unfading light, sparkling like the dawn, and glittering in the full radiance of the sun. Its foundations rest on fallen stones that God has restored and rejointed. The walls shimmer with precious living stones, and its windows are of topaz and sapphire. Its towers are glimmering gold shining brightly in the brilliant radiance of the blessed, and within it the Holy Spirit plays and sings.

Life lay hidden in the midst of the Almighty. It continued like that in silence until the brilliant white cloud that had been veiled for so long shone forth. Then the dawn broke and flowed about the sun. And the sun emitted its rays and built a great city. It brought forth twelve lights, and in the third phase of sleep it awakened those who had been in a deep slumber. Then all the eagles that dwelled in the brilliant white cloud were suffused with light and looked out on all that happened....

And so the new world that emerged from the waters appeared in a fiery light that flowed about the mountains and hills. And now the whole cosmos sings the same song that angels sang.

(LMV IV, 31)

74. The City of God
The buildings represent the construction of the "Golden City" in the course of the history of salvation. The Dove over the mountain stands for divine Providence in the unfolding of that history toward a salvation already accepted by the angels, whereas humanity is still maturing to that point.
Liber Divinorum Operum, c. 1140; Ms 1942, Lucca, Biblioteca Statale

Saving actions

Hildegard's three great visions close with her account of the end of the world and of the appearance of the cosmic Christ. In *Scivias* the Son of Man appears on the Last Day, the Day of Final Revelation, in order to inhabit the New Heaven and the New Earth together with the redeemed human race. In the *Liber Divinorum Operum* the five great Last Ages announce the coming of Christ over his transfigured world. Finally, the *Liber Vitae Meritorum* (Book of Divine Merits) describes the joys of the blessed who dwell in the true homeland of the transfigured cosmos.

"For God labours continuously over his works until all the elect are fulfilled in heavenly harmony. God continually watches over and tends this harmony, which will last for ever" (LDO IX, 9). Everything is directed to the Son, who issued from the Father's heart and became human to exert all his loving vigour and thus redeem the world. Everything is oriented to the cosmic Christ.

Everything in the world is in process and movement as it advances toward salvation: nature, epochs, and human beings, who, as they move forward and the wheel of time turns, must decide of their own free will where they are going. They must choose Christ as their goal and purpose, for he assumed human nature in order to transform all the inadequacies and mishaps of creation into holy and heavenly matter, according to the mighty power whereby he is able to subdue all things unto himself. By the burgeoning, fruitful vigour of the evolving cosmos (LVM I, 23: *prosperitas egrediendi*) and by the strength of the universal life-force (*viriditas mundi*), everything grows and develops until it is in a state of infinite transfiguration (*transmutatio indeficiens*). God's Word shines out in human form (*clarescit in forma hominis*), and humans are reflected in the Word, for we all contribute to the formation of his glorious body (Pi 458: *aedificantes membra sui pulchri corporis*).

"And so the Spirit sweeps through the universe with resounding, inspiring, and igniting power, evoking the response of renewed vitality until the last day. This is the purpose and action of God, who has no beginning and no end. He created humanity as the wonderful work of his hands by equipping people with an impulse and inclination to higher things, and by enabling them to make their own responses. God did this because he loved people. After all, he is Love itself."

The "bright flowers on the glorious body of the Son of God" are now at the pitch of perfection. They are fit and able to return in full physical form to the Father's heart, in order to live in the place and way in which they were intended to exist: in the wholeness of their bodies. "For even the blessed in heaven cannot enjoy perfect happiness as long as they are separated from their physical selves. They still have an irrepressible inward longing for the bodies that will enable them, as their innermost impulses tell them, to achieve an even greater level of joy for ever" (LVM V, 63).

"But as soon as they themselves have regained their bodies and have become their own whole and undivided selves, they are able to perceive and experience salvation in all its uttermost perfect infinity, focussed as it now is on Perfection itself. After that they are truly wholesome and can never change or be changed again" (LVM I, 42). Only with the resurrection of the dead will all be made alive. Then their bodies will all be changed, in a moment, in the twinkling of an eye, and they will live unchangeably for ever.

75. The Soul leaving its Body
Figures of light and darkness are angels and demons disputing possession of the soul leaving its physical shell for eternity.

Detail, Liber Scivias, copy of the former Rupertsberg Codex, *c.* 1180; St Hildegard's Abbey, Eibingen

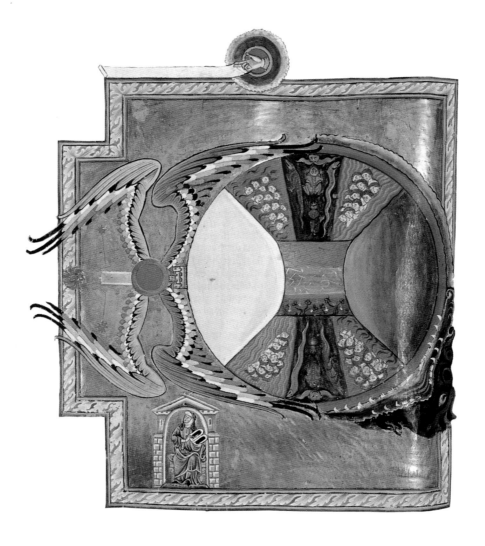

Hildegard the visionary peers out from this world into the infinite spaces of the life hereafter, where all human effort is rewarded and acquires its definitive form in a dimension of refinement and purification. Her picture of the world is conceived geometrically. The habitable human earth lies at its centre. It is surrounded by high mountains and has four divisions and three areas. The eastmost arc is bright and is the realm of the blessed, whereas the westmost section is dark and represents the place of retribution where sinners dwell. The five regions signify the five senses by which people enact their humanity and are enabled to save their souls. The intense red sphere enclosed in a sapphire circle indicates that God's insistence on expiation is enforced not only by justice but by love, and is maintained by the wings of divine Providence, which incline toward each other in infinity.

76. The Realms of the Next Life
Liber Divinorum Operum, *c.* 1240; Ms 1942, Lucca, Biblioteca Statale

77. The Day of Judgment

At the end of the ages a cleansing storm will come upon the earth. All the elements and all creatures will be in turmoil. The Son of Man with open wounds will appear in a cloud, accompanied by angels bearing the instruments of his passion. The world will await God's judgment with foreboding.

Liber Scivias, copy of the former Rupertsberg Codex, c. 1180; St Hildegard's Abbey, Eibingen

"The dead will be raised up to eternal life as physical beings" (LVM I, 64). Now our human flesh still holds the spirit imprisoned in the body: "But then the spirit will control its body, and people will be entirely holy."

When the ages draw to a close, the Golden City of God is finally built, and the body has been glorified, a stage beyond the transfiguration of nature will be reached with the dawning of the long-expected era of peace. "In those days the most exquisite clouds and tender breezes will gently touch the earth until it is filled to overflowing with fresh life, fertility, and abundance. Then people will experience the justice that the world so sadly lacked in the age of effeminate weakness. Together with their rulers, the whole population of the earth will rearrange God's ordinances in a new dispensation. All weapons, manufactured for purposes of death and destruction, will be forbidden and the only tools, devices, and machinery permitted will be those that serve the cultivation of the land and are truly useful to humankind" (LDO X, 20).

But when the end of all ages arrives, all the elements will be unleashed and people will find themselves drawn along in a furiously dramatic and general commotion. Fire will break out, the waters will overflow, the air will be in turmoil, lightning will crack, thunder will resound, the mountains will split, the forests will collapse, and everything mortal will breathe its last. Yet this cosmic convulsion is intended to purify everything, for all that is ugly, hateful, and vile will vanish from the face of the earth as if it had never been (Sc III, 12).

On the day of the last great Revelation the new world will appear, totally transformed. All its elements will be purified. All human bones will rise up and in the twinkling of an eye will once again be adorned with their flesh. "And all people will rise up again. There they will stand with their limbs and bodies unharmed, all in their appropriate gender (*integris membris et corporibus suis in sexo suo*)" (Sc III, 12).

"And all the elements will suddenly shine out in their full splendour, as if a black skin had been peeled off them. The fire will cease, turbulence will peter out in the atmosphere, the water will stop boiling, and the earth will be firm and imperishable. The sun, moon, and stars will shine and sparkle in the firmament with their full lustre, and they will be most beautiful to behold. They will stand still where formerly they moved along their preordained paths, and there will be no day or night. There will be universal day, for night will have ceased for ever. The end will have come" (Sc III, 12).

At the end of time the forces of the cosmos will be cleansed from all wretchedness and melancholy and will shine forth with a new brilliance. Freed from the burden of earthly elements, human beings too will be like the circumference of a golden wheel (*aureus circulus rotae*). "They will be purified in body and in soul; they will have reached maturity; and all the deepest mysteries will be revealed to them. God will let them rejoice and they will be fulfilled (*plenum gaudium*)" (LVM VI, 17). Then the whole world will exist in the full beauty of vitality and freshness (*pulchritudo viriditatis*) (LDO IV, 12).

The joy of a happy life in loving harmony will be the ultimate image of the world, for it will be the newly composed and sweetly tuned wedding music of perfect unison (*canticum novum omnis caelestis harmoniae*). The covenant between God and humanity will be concluded anew and last for ever. For Love made the world, and now Love has brought everything to completion and reigns supreme in the image and reality of what God has wrought in his creation, humankind.

The hymn of love

Now the great hymn of love resounds anew and life rejoices continually. Love is here as it was before all time began and is in eternity, in the full power of the Godhead, in order to conduct the blessed to their eternal home, "to the full glory of heavenly joy." The glory of the new Paradise flowers in the vitality of greenness and beauty, for here the blessed "body and soul enjoy their happiness": the "splendour and joyous delights of heavenly wonders that no human can perceive."

Love has its dwelling-place in eternity. "For when God decided to make the world he bent down to express his inexpressibly tender love. He foresaw everything that was needed for life, just as a father prepares an inheritance for his son. And so he formed all his works in an ardent outpouring of his love." Accordingly, love was already there in the very ground of the world. The whole creation was the work of love. God clothed humankind out of love. "It was love that made the human race; and it was humility that redeemed it. And hope was there too, as the very eye of love. Love is there, for it is everlasting and has no end" (Bw 140-142).

God's being is perfect love. Of its very nature love does not want to stay there in itself, self-enclosed and undistributed. It longs to emerge and to break its own bounds, to share with another, and communicate itself. Love shapes itself and all its ways in relations and encounters. God himself is not a hidden fire. He is an active, not a secret, flickering flame. He is fire seeking a response. "God made rational life so that the eyes might see, the ears hear, the nose smell, and the mouth utter words of reason."

Love is not satisfied with itself but is impelled toward another being. It does not exist in self-regard but looks for and to the other who is dear to it. It is committed to an other, offers reliability and trust to an other, and opens itself to an other. Love is always totally committed to the beloved and will always persist to the end. It longs for and demands fulfilment of its loving self. "For this reason, the basic impulse of humans too is directed entirely outward, toward love."

By their nature, then, human beings should be attuned to the tenderness of love (*dulcedo dilectionis*) of God, and should also love themselves (*diligens se ipsum*). "For when you love God you also love your own salvation (*Si diligis Deum, diligis salutem tuum*)." And if you love and respect yourself in all respects, then you should also love your neighbour (Sc III, 8).

It was within this scope and in this context that God made the world, out of perfect love. In the beginning the loving heart dwelled in the Father's breast. Its light was inspired by the fire of love and flamed up and resounded in the Word. A world of love became apparent in the Word, and the heart became living Spirit. This Word became human. Now the verdant heart of humankind exists in the midst of this world. The loving work of the Father in the Word-and-Body of the Son is the vital force of the Spirit's heart (*opus verbi viriditas*). Human beings are not merely invited guests at the meal of creation. They have been made partners in the trinitarian banquet and dialogue.

Love is the "innermost power, the very breath of the Father's loving heart." The tender expressions of love flow over all aspects of existence. Love is lovingly inclined (*amantissima*) to all that is. The Incarnation of God's own Son is the fruit of its loving action. And the fiery Spirit of love flows over the entire world: "surging from the most profound depths to encompass even the brightest star," and pouring over every light in the firmament. God's love fills the human heart to overflowing.

Hildegard's images of love are supported by a clear and consistent idea. God produced his Son in the generosity of his fatherly love. God's Word became flesh and inspirited the world. The origin of love is entirely trinitarian: in the original resonance of the Father, in the Son's resounding Word, and in the spiritual breath of the fire of Reason. The whole universe is suffused with love (S 36: *caritas abundat in omnia*).

It is not the head but the heart that is the main organ of reason. The heart is the gateway to the world, for the core and essence of the universe is the love of which it may be said: "Whoever understands its true nature will look neither above nor to either side, for love is always at the centre of things" (Sc III, 13). Love does not overthrow or destroy because it is the core of all that is. The